The Wanderings
of Clare Skymer

GEORGE MACDONALD (1824-1905) was a Scottish preacher, novelist, and poet. He wrote more than fifty books, including the classic fantasies *At the Back of the North Wind, The Princess and the Goblin,* and *The Princess and Curdie.*

The story of Clare Skymer originally appeared in 1889 as *A Rough Shaking,* a once-popular novel which has been lost for 75 years.

A revised edition of *A Rough Shaking* was prepared in 1986 by Dan Hamilton, who has edited several other George MacDonald novels.

Winner Books has abridged and adapted Mr. Hamilton's edition to produce *The Wanderings of Clare Skymer,* specifically for the enjoyment of today's young readers.

The Wanderings of Clare Skymer

GEORGE MACDONALD

A WINNER BOOK

VICTOR BOOKS™
A DIVISION OF SCRIPTURE PRESS PUBLICATIONS INC.
USA CANADA ENGLAND

WINNER BOOKS BY GEORGE MACDONALD:
The Boyhood of Ranald Bannerman
The Genius of Willie MacMichael
The Wanderings of Clare Skymer

Library of Congress Catalog Card Number: 86-63160
ISBN: 0-89693-757-7

VICTOR BOOKS
A division of SP Publications, Inc.
Wheaton, Illinois 60187

CONTENTS

PROLOGUE

It was June—one of those almost perfect days when everything around comes nearly right for a moment or two, preparing to come all right for good at the last. I was walking through the thin edge of a little woods of big trees when I heard the strong, sweet tones of a man's voice talking to someone. The voice was deep and musical, with something like coaxing in it, and something like tenderness, and the intent of it puzzled me.

The wood abruptly opened to a field—divided from both the woods and the path by a fence of three bars. On one side of the fence stood a man whose face I could not see; on the other side was one of the loveliest horses I had ever set my eyes upon. He was over sixteen hands, with a small head and broad muzzle; hollows above his eyes of hazy blue revealed his advanced age. Neither the man nor the horse heard my approach. The man had his arm around the horse's neck, and was caressing his face, talking to him in a musical baritone.

Then the horse saw me. He gave a little start, threw up his head, uttered a shrill neigh of warning, then stepped back a pace and stood motionless, waiting apparently for an order from his master.

The man looked around, saw me, lifted his hat, and advanced a step as if to welcome a guest. He looked around sixty years of age. His face was of the palest health, with a faint light from within. His hair and beard, both rather long, were quite white. His face was wonderfully handsome, with the stillness of a summer sea upon it, and his friendly eyes

7

were light hazel. Though slender in build, he looked strong, and every movement denoted activity.

"I fear I have intruded!" I said.

The man laughed—and his laugh was more friendly than an invitation to dinner. "The land is mine," he answered. "No one can say you intrude. You are welcome to go where you will on my property."

He turned from me, and as if to introduce a companion, he called, "Memnon, come!" At once the animal walked up to the rails, rose gently on his hind legs, came over without touching, walked up to his master, and laid his head on his shoulder.

I knew who he was. Clare Skymer had been but a year or two in the neighborhood, and his neighbors all agreed he was a very peculiar person. People believed he had gradually lost hold of what sense he might at one time have possessed. But I could hardly count a man beside himself because he was a friend with his horse.

"Pardon my rude lingering," I said. "That lovely animal is enough to make one desire nearer acquaintance with his owner. I don't think I ever saw such a perfect creature!"

"I grant him nearly a perfect creature," he answered, "but he is far more nearly perfect than you know! Excuse me for speaking so confidently—but if we were half as far on for men as Memnon is for a horse, the kingdom of heaven would be a good deal nearer! Come here, Memnon!"

The horse, who had been standing behind like a servant in waiting, bent his neck to his master.

"Memnon," said Mr. Skymer, "go home and tell Mrs. Waterhouse I hope to bring a gentleman with me to lunch."

The horse walked gently past us, then started at a quick trot, which almost immediately became a gallop.

"The dear fellow would not gallop like that if he were on the hard road," said his master. "He knows I would not like it."

"But how can he convey your message?"

"The housekeeper will look in his mane for the knot

which I tied in it. I have a code of signals by knots—and I hope you do not object to the message! You will do me the honor of lunching with me?"

"You are most kind," I answered, though with a little hesitation.

"Don't make me false to horse and housekeeper," he resumed. "I put the horse first, because I could more easily explain the thing to Mrs. Waterhouse than to Memnon."

"Could you explain it to Memnon?"

"I should have a try!" he answered, with a peculiar smile. "A word understood is binding, whether spoken to horse or man or pig. It seems to me an absolute horror that a man should lie to the lower animals. Just think—if an angel were to lie to us! What a shock to find we had been reposing faith in a devil—for when he lied, would he not be a devil? But let us follow Memnon, and as we walk I will tell you more about him."

We walked a score or two yards in silence before he resumed. "I delight in talking about my poor brothers and sisters! Most of them are only savages yet, but there would be far fewer such if we did not treat them as slaves instead of friends. One day, however, all will be well for them as for us—thank God."

"I hope so," I responded heartily. "But what a loss it will be to you when he dies!"

He looked grave for an instant, then replied cheerfully, "Of course, I shall miss the dear fellow, but not more than he will miss me. And it will be good for both of us."

"Then," said I, a little startled, I confess, "you really think—"

"Do *you* think," he rejoined, "that a God like Jesus Christ would invent such a delight for His children as the society and love of animals, and then let death part them forever? I don't, though I know I can't give a shadow of proof for my theory! I never was the fool to imagine I could—but as surely as you go to bed at night expecting to rise again in the morning, so surely do I expect to see my dear old

Memnon again when I wake from what so many Christians call 'the sleep that knows no waking.'"

We walked in silence to the other side of the small wood. There stood Memnon, with his neck stretched toward us over a paling that fenced the wood from a well-kept country road.

"Memnon," said Mr. Skymer as we went by the gate, "I want you to carry this gentleman home."

I did not relish mounting Memnon without either saddle or bridle—but there he lay at my feet, flat as his equine rotundity would permit. Ashamed of my doubt, I placed myself astride him, and he rose and lifted me—then he looked round at his master, and we set off at a leisurely pace.

Our procession of horse and foot went about a half-mile before anything more was said worth setting down. Then we obviously began drawing nigh to a house: first came trees in the hedgerows, and then the hedges gave way to trees—a grand avenue of splendid elms and beeches.

"Where, may I ask, does Memnon come from?"

"He was born in England, the son of a Syrian mare and an English thoroughbred. He was born into my arms, and for a week never touched the ground. Next month he will be forty years old!"

"It is a great age for a horse!" I said.

"The more the shame as well as the pity!" he answered.

"Then you think horses might live longer?"

"Much longer than they are allowed to live in this country," he answered. "And a part of our punishment is that we do not know them. We treat them so selfishly that they do not live long enough to become our friends. It is a small wonder there should be so many stupid horses, when they receive so little education, have such bad associates, and die too young to have gained any ripe experience to transmit to their posterity. Where would humanity be now if we all died before twenty-five?"

"I think you must be right. I had a pony that died at the

age of at least forty-two, and did her part of the work of a pair till within a year or two of her death. Poor little Zephyr!"

"You talk of her as if she were a Christian!" exclaimed Mr. Skymer.

"That's how you talked of Memnon a moment ago!"

"I didn't say *poor Memnon,* did I? You said *poor Zephyr!* That is the way Christians talk about their friends gone home. But here we are at the gate! Call, Memnon."

The horse gave a clear whinny, gentle, but loud enough to be heard at some distance. It was a tall gate of wrought iron, but Memnon's summons was answered by one who could clear it, though not open it: a little bird fluttered down and perched on top of the gate, then dropped suddenly on Memnon's left ear, and then to his master's shoulder, where he sat till the gate was opened.

The boy who opened the gate, a chubby little fellow of seven, looked up in Mr. Skymer's face as if he had been his father and king in one, and stood gazing after him as long as he was in sight.

Every now and then another bird would drop from a tree, and alight for a minute on my host's head. At one point seven or eight perched together on it, and one tiny bird got caught in his beard by the claws.

"You cannot surely have tamed *all* the birds in your grounds!" I said.

"If I have," he answered, "it has been by permitting them to be themselves."

"You mean it is the nature of birds to be friendly with man?"

"I do. Through long ages men have been their enemies, and so have alienated them."

The avenue led to a wide graveled space before a plain low, long building in a whitish stone, with pillared portico. In the middle of the space was a fountain, and close to it a few chairs. Memnon walked up to the fountain and lay down, that I might get off his back as easily as I had got on it. Once down, he turned on his side and lay still.

"The air is so mild," said my host, "I fancy you will prefer this to the house."

"Mild!" I rejoined. "I should call it hot!"

"I have been so much in real heat!" he returned. "Notwithstanding my love of turf, I keep this much gravel for the sake of the desert."

I took the seat he offered me. My host went to the other side of the basin, and suddenly a great uprush of water spread above us like a tent-like dome, through which the sun came with a cool, broken, frosty glitter. I exclaimed with delight.

"I thought you would enjoy my sunshade!" said Mr. Skymer. "Memnon and I often come here on a hot morning, when nobody wants us."

We had not been seated many moments when we were interrupted by the invasion of half a dozen dogs. Mr. Skymer called one of them Tadpole—I suppose because he had the hugest tail, while his legs were hardly visible.

"That animal," said his master, "looks like a dog, but who would be positive what he is! He is the cleverest in the pack, and a rare individual. His ancestors must have been of all sorts, and he has gathered from them every good quality possessed by each. Think what a man might be—made up that way!"

"Why is there no such man?" I asked.

"There may be some such men. There must be many one day, but not for a while yet. Men must first be made willing to be noble."

"And you don't think men are willing to be made noble?"

"Oh, yes! They are willing enough *to be made* noble, but that is very different from being willing *to be* noble—that takes trouble. How can anyone become noble who desires it so little as not to fight for it!"

The man had a way of talking about things seldom mentioned except in dull fashion in the pulpit, as if he cared about them. He spoke as of familiar things, but made you feel he was looking out of a high window.

I sat for a while, gazing up through the fine veil of water at the blue sky so far beyond. I thought of what my host had said concerning the too short lives of horses, and wondered what he would say about those of dogs.

"Dogs are more intelligent than horses," I said. "Why do they live a yet shorter time?"

"If you had said, 'still more affectionate,' I should have said that is just why they live no longer. They do not find the world good enough for them, die, and leave it."

"They have a much happier life than horses!"

"Many dogs than some horses, I grant."

That instant arose what I fancied must be an unusual sound in the place: two of the dogs were fighting. The master got up, and I thought I should see his notions of discipline. In his hand was a small riding whip, which I afterward found he always carried in avoidance of having to inflict a heavier punishment from inability to inflict a lighter. He held that in all wrongdoing man can deal with, the kindest thing is not only to punish, but to punish at once. He ran to the conflicting parties, who separated before him. One came cringing and crawling to his feet, while the other—Tadpole—stood a little way off, wagging his tail, and cocking his head up in his master's face. He gave the one at his feet several strokes with the whip, and sent him off. The other drew nearer, but his master turned away and took no notice of him.

"May I ask," I said, when he returned, "why you did not punish both the animals for their breach of the peace?"

"They did not both deserve it."

"How could you tell that? You were not looking when the quarrel began!"

"Ah, but you see I know the dogs! Tadpole had found a bone, and dog rule is that what you find is yours. But the other wanted a share. Tadpole—partly from his sense of justice—cannot endure to have his claims infringed upon. Every dog of them knows that Tadpole must be in the right."

"He looked as if he expected you to approve of his conduct!"

"Yes, that is the worst of Tadpole. He is so self-righteous as to imagine he deserves praise for standing on his rights! He is but a dog, you see, and knows no better. I disregarded his appeal because I will not praise him for nothing!"

"You expect them to understand your treatment?"

"No one can tell how infinitesimally small the beginnings of understanding, as of life, may be. The only way to make animals more reasonable is to treat them as reasonable. Until you can go down into the abysses of creation, you cannot know *when* a nature begins to see a difference in quality of action."

"Tadpole *did* seem a little ashamed as he went away."

"And you see Blanco White at my feet, taking care not to touch them. He is giving time, he thinks, for my anger to pass." He laughed the merriest laugh. The dog looked up eagerly, but dropped his head again.

I was drawn to the man as seldom to another. I was greatly his inferior, but love is a quick divider of shares: he that gathers much has nothing over, and he that gathers little has no lack. I soon ceased to think of him as my *new* friend, for I seemed to have known him before I was born. He never told me any great portion of the tale of his life continuously, but I have pieced the parts together, and will tell the history of his childhood—beginning many long years ago, in a small village in a corner of Italy.

CHAPTER ONE
A Rough Shaking

The long, lingering dinner was just over in one of the inns on the cornice road. The gentlemen had gone into the garden, and some of the ladies to the sitting room, where open windows admitted the odors of many a flower and blossoming tree, for it was toward the end of spring in that region. The twilight had speedily thickened into night, and its darkness was filled with thousands of fireflies. A tall, graceful Englishwoman stood in one of the windows alone. Mrs. Skymer had never been to Italy before, had never before seen fireflies, and was absorbed in the beauty of their motion and the golden flashes of the roving stars.

She gave a little sigh and looked around, regretting that her husband was not by her side to look on the loveliness that woke a faint-hued fairy tale in her heart. The same moment Harry Skymer entered the room and came to her. He was the commander of an English gunboat, which he was now on his way to Genoa to join. He was in his twenties, though his face was browned by sun and wind.

His wife was delicate, lovely, and very fair, with large deep-blue eyes. They had been married about five years. A friend had brought them in his yacht as far as Nice, and they were now going on by land. From Genoa the lady would make her way home without her husband.

The lights in the room were dimmed that they might better see the fireflies, and he put his arm around her waist.

"I'm so glad you're here, Harry!" she said. "I was uncomfortable at having the lovely sight all to myself!"

"It is lovely, darling!" he rejoined. "I hope you will be able to sleep without the sea to rock you!"

"No fear of that!" she answered. "The stillness will be delightful."

"I am glad you like the change. I never sleep the first night on shore."

"Never mind, love. I will stay awake with you."

"In the meantime, let's fetch Clare to see the fireflies."

She left the room. Her husband stood where he was, gazing out with a tender look on his face that deepened to sadness—perhaps from the thought of his wife's delicate health and his having to leave her. When she returned with their one child in her arms, he hurried to take him from her.

The child was a fair, bright boy. The sleep in his eyes had turned to wonder, for they seemed to see everything, and be quite satisfied with nothing. In his delight with the fireflies, he looked now to his mother, now to his father, speechless, with shining eyes.

The father turned to carry him back to bed, and the woman's eyes fell upon two or three delicate, small-leaved plants that stood in pots on the balcony in front of the open window. The night was perfectly still, but the leaves were trembling.

"Look, Harry! What is that?" she cried, pointing to them.

"It must be some loaded wagon passing," he said, and went off with the child.

"I hope tomorrow will be just like today!" said his wife when he returned. "What shall we do with it? It's our one real holiday, you know!"

"That little town we heard of—Graffiacane—is among the hills not far from here. Shall we go and see it?"

*****

Another English couple—a country parson and his wife— were abroad for the first time in their now middle-age lives. Attended by a guide and borne by donkeys, the Porsons were slowly climbing a steep terraced and zigzagged road, with olive trees above and below them. They were on the south side of the hill, and the olives gave them little shadow.

The man often wiped his red, innocent face, and looked distressed; but the lady, although as stout as he, did not seem to suffer, perhaps because she was sheltered by a very large bonnet.

The speed they made was small—but it was a festa,* and hot. They were on the way to Graffiacane on the crest of the hill they were now ascending.

Numerous were the sharp turns the donkeys made in their ascent; and at this corner and that, the sweetest life-giving wind would leap out upon the travellers, as if it had been lying there in wait to surprise them. But they were getting too tired to enjoy anything, and were both indeed not far from asleep on the backs of their humble beasts when they saw before them the little town.

Passing through the narrow arch of the low-browed gateway, hot as was the hour, a sudden cold struck to their bones. For not a ray of light shone into the narrow street. Narrow, rough, steep old stone stairs ran up between and inside the lofty houses, all the doors of which were open to the air—here, however, none of the sweetest. Everywhere was shadow; everywhere one or another evil odor; everywhere a look of abject and dirty poverty—to an English eye, that is. Everywhere were pretty children, young, slatternly mothers, and withered-up grandmothers. As it was a festa, more men than usual were looking out of cavern-like doorways or over handwrought iron balconies, were leaning their backs against the doorposts, and smoking as if too lazy to stop. Many of the women were at prayers in the church.

The sides of the streets were connected, at the height of two or perhaps three stories, by thin arches—mere jets of stone from the one house to the other, with nothing to keep down the key of the arch. They had straddled there undisturbed long enough for moss and even grass to grow upon

---

*You can find an explanation of the starred words in the Glossary, pages 166-167.

them. Mr. Porson summoned what Italian he could, supplemented it with Latin and an *o* or *a* tacked to any French or English word that offered help, and succeeded in gathering from a bystander that the arches were there because of the earthquakes.

Turning away to tell his wife what he had learned, he was checked by a low rumbling. The next instant the Porsons felt the ground under their feet move up and down and from side to side with confused motion. A sudden great cry arose, and down every stair and out of every door, like animals from their holes, came men and women and children with a rush. The earthquake was upon them.

But in such narrow streets, the danger could hardly be less than inside the houses, some of which were ill constructed with boulder-stones that had neither angles nor edges, hence little grasp on each other beyond what the friction of their weight and the adhesion of their poor old friable cement gave them. After about twenty seconds of shaking, the lonely pair began to hear some such houses rumbling to the earth.

They were far more bewildered than frightened. They did not know the danger they were in. For one moment many of the inhabitants stood in the street motionless, pale, and staring; the next they all began to run, some for the gateway, but the greater part up the street, staggering as they ran.

They had not run far, however, before the terrible unrest ceased as suddenly as it had begun. The English pair drew a long breath where they stood—for they had not stirred a step, or indeed thought where to run—and imagining it over for a hundred years, looked around them. Their guide had disappeared. The two dejected donkeys stood perfectly still with their heads hanging down. A few men only were yet running up the street, hurrying to join their women in the one safe place in town—the church.

The Porsons followed them to an open *piazza,** on the upper side of which rose the great church. It had a square front like a screen, masking the triangular gable of the building. Upon this screen, in the brightest of colors, was represented the day of judgment—the mother seated on the right hand of the judge, and casting a pitiful look upon the miserable assembly on her left. The last tatters of the crowd disappeared through the great church door, and but for the Porsons the square was empty. As they went slowly up to the church, they kept looking at the picture.

All at once the huge building began to shudder. The tiles on the roof began to clatter and the ground began to wriggle and heave. Down came the plaster surface, with the judge and his mother, clashing on the pavement below, while the good and the bad yet stood trembling. Then there came a roaring crash and a huge rumbling, through and far above which, rose a shriek of terror, dismay, and agony, and a number of men and women issued as if shot from a catapult. A few people came straggling out behind them, and then no more. The roof had fallen upon the rest.

The shaking ceased, and the still earth seemed again immovable. In the air there was a cloud of dust so thick as to look almost solid, and from the cloud came a ghastly cry of shrieks and groans and appeals for help.

The stunned Porsons came to their senses and entered the building. With white faces and trembling hands, they drew aside the heavy leather curtain that hung within the great door, but could for a moment see nothing: the air inside seemed filled with a solid yellow dust. As their eyes recovered from the sudden change of sunlight for gloom, however, they perceived that the floor was one confused heap of rafters and bricks and tiles and stones and lime. The center of the roof had been a great dome—but now there was nothing between their eyes and the clear heaven except the slowly vanishing cloud of ruin.

In the mound below they could at first distinguish nothing human—could not have told limbs from broken rafters in the dim chaos. Eager to help, they dared not set their feet upon the mass, lest their own added weight should crush someone beneath. Three or four rescuers were moving about the edges of the heap, vaguely trying to lift now this, now that, but yielding each attempt in despair. They would give a pull at a beam that lay across some writhing figure, find it immovable, and turn with a groan to some farther cry. How or where were they to help? Others began to come in with white faces and terror-stricken eyes, and before long the sepulchral ruin had little groups all over it, endeavoring in shiftless fashion to bring rescue to the prisoned souls.

The Porsons saw nothing they could do. Great beams and rafters beyond their power lay across in all directions, and they could hold little communication with those who were in a fashion at work. The two saw more plainly now, and could distinguish contorted limbs, and here and there a countenance. The silence was itself growing terrible. Had they known how many were buried there, they would have wondered so few were left able to cry out.

The heart of Mrs. Porson began to sink. "Do come out," she whispered, sick and faint, and afraid of her own voice. As she spoke something touched her leg, and she gave a cry and started aside. It was a hand, but of the body to which it belonged nothing could be seen. It must have been its last movement, for now it stuck there motionless. Then they spied amid sad sights a sadder still: upon the heap, a little way from its edge, sat a child of about three, dressed like a sailor, gazing down at something. Going a little nearer, they saw a fair English woman, lying dead with a great beam across her heart. The child's white face was tearless and frozen, and pity drove Mrs. Porson's sickness away.

"My dear!" she said. The child took no heed, but her voice seemed to wake something in him. He started to his feet, rushed at the beam, and began to tug at it with his tiny hands. Mrs. Porson burst into tears. "It's no use, darling!" she cried.

"Wake, Mamma!" he said, turning, and looking up at her.

"She will not wake," sobbed Mrs. Porson.

"She *will* wake," returned the boy. "She always wakes when I kiss her."

He knelt beside her white face, where he had already kissed away much of the dust, though none of the death. When once more he found that she did not even close her lips to return his passionate salute, he desisted. With that saddest of things, a child's sigh, and a look that seemed to Mrs. Porson to embody the riddle of humanity, he reseated himself on the beam, with his little feet on his mother's bosom. He did not weep, nor did he fix his eyes on his mother; his look was level and moveless and set upon nothing.

"Where is your papa?" asked Mr. Porson.

The boy looked bewildered. "Gone," he answered.

"Was your papa with you here?" asked Mrs. Porson.

He answered only with the dazed word *gone*.

By this time all the men in the town were doing their best. They had already pulled one or two people out alive, and their own priest dead. They worked well, their terror of the lurking earthquake forgotten in their eagerness to rescue. From their own ignorance of the language, however, Mr. Porson saw that they themselves could be of little use.

They stood one moment and looked at each other in silence. The child had dropped from the beam, and lay fast asleep across his mother's bosom, with his head on a lump of mortar. Without a word, Mrs. Porson picked her way to the spot, knelt down by the dead mother, tenderly kissed her cheek, lifted the sleeping child, and with all the awe, and nearly all the tremulous joy of first motherhood, bore him to her husband. In silent agreement, they turned and left the crumbled church.

When they turned into the street that led to the gate, they found the donkeys standing where they had left them. Their owner was not with them, for he too had perished in the church. When they caught sight of the patient, dejected animals, unheeded and unheeding, then first they spoke, whispering in the awful stillness of the world: they must take the creatures, and make the best of their way back without a guide.

Not a person was in the street when they mounted; almost all had been trapped in the church. Mrs. Porson mounted the strongest of the animals, her husband placed the sleeping child in her arms, and they started. They were not sure of the way, but so long as they went downward, and did not leave the road, they could hardly go wrong. The child slept all the way.

No conceivable treasure of the world could have compared with the burden of richness Mrs. Porson bore. As they went down one of the hills, she slept for a moment, and dreamed that she was Mary with the holy child in her arms, fleeing to Egypt on the ass, with Joseph by her side. For years and years they had been longing for a child—and here lay the divinest little one, with every mark of the kingdom upon him! With his father and mother lying crushed under the fallen dome of that fearful church, was it strange he should seem to belong to her?

But there might be someone somewhere in the world with a better claim—possibly with more need of him than she! Up started a fierce temptation, such as she had never imagined. We do not know what is in us until temptation comes. Then there is the devil to fight, and Mrs. Porson fought him.

Mr. Porson could not help wishing, nor was he wrong in wishing that, since the child's father and mother were gone, they might take their place, and love their orphan. They were far from rich, but what was one child! They might surely manage to give him a good education, and set him doing for himself! But, alas, there might be others with love-property in the child! The same thoughts were working in each, but neither dared utter them in the presence of the sleeping treasure.

They travelled slowly on through a dying sunset and an hour or two of the star-bright night that followed, adorned rather than lighted by a crescent moon. Weary, but rapt in a voiceless triumph, they came at last to their hotel.

All there were talking of the earthquake, and even after the Porsons were inside there came two or three small and separate shocks. Every time, out with a cry rushed the inhabitants into the streets. But the little couple, who had that day seen so much more of its terrors than anyone else in the place, and whose chamber was at the top of the house where the swaying was worst, were too much absorbed in watching and tending the orphan boy to heed the earthquake.

"If his father and mother are permitted to see their child," said Mrs. Porson, as they stood regarding him, "they shall see how we love him, and be willing he should love us!"

As they went up the stairs with the boy, he woke. When he looked and saw a face that was not his mother's, a cloud swept across the heaven of his eyes. He closed them again, and did not speak. The first of the shocks came as they were putting him to bed: he turned very white and looked up fixedly, as if waiting another fall from above, but sat motionless on his new mother's lap. The instant the vibration and rocking ceased, he drank quietly from the cup of milk she offered him. When she put him in the bed, he looked at her with such an expression of bewildered loss that she burst into tears. The child did not cry—had not cried since they took him. The woman's heart was like to break for him, but she managed to say, "God has taken her, my darling. He is keeping her for you, and I am going to keep you for her," and with that she kissed him.

The boy fell fast asleep, and never woke till the morning. Mrs. Porson lay beside him, though scarcely sleeping.

The Porsons were honest people, and for all their desire to possess the child, made no secret of how and where they had found him, or of as much of his name as he could tell them, which was only *Clare*. But they never heard of any inquiry after him.

The crew of the gunboat at Genoa grew uneasy about their absent commander, and made a fruitless search for him.

CHAPTER TWO
A New Home

The part of England to which the Porsons carried the gift of the earthquake had no very distinctive features. It had many fields in crop, and some lying fallow in grass—all softly undulating. It had some trees, and everywhere hedges dividing fields whose strange shapes witnessed to a complicated history.

It was the very country for the boy. Clare would come into more contact with its modest beauty in a day than some of us would in a year. The winds that blew upon little Clare were more often filled with the smell of farmyards, and burning weeds, and cottage-fires, than that of flowers; but never would one of such odors revisit him without bringing fresh delight to his heart.

There was a very small village in the parish, and a good many farmhouses.

The parsonage was old, and swallows had loved it for centuries. It had a very old garden, nearly as old-fashioned as it was old, and many flowers that have almost ceased to be seen grew in it, and did not enjoy their lives the less that they were out of fashion. All the furniture was old, and mostly shabby; it was possible, therefore, to love it a little.

Clare's new father and mother had a charming little room made for him in the garret, right up among the swallows, who soon admitted him a member of their society.

His new parents saw that when he could not be with them, he preferred being by himself, and that moods came upon him in which he would steal away even from them, seized with a longing for loneliness. In general, next to being with his mother anywhere, he liked to be with his father in the study. If both went out, and could not take him with them, he would either go to his own room, or sit in the study alone.

His mother often sat in a tiny little drawing room, which smelled of withered rose leaves. Clare loved the smell of the rose leaves, yet he preferred the study with its dingy books to the pretty drawing room without his mother.

Such was the place in which Clare spent the next few years of his life, and there his new parents loved him heartily. The only thing that troubled them was that they could not draw out the tiniest smile upon Clare's sweet, moonlight face.

Mr. Porson was about forty-five, and his wife was a few years younger. He tried constantly to obey the law of God, whether he found it in the Bible or in his own heart. He never wrote or read a sermon, but talked to his people as one who would meet what was in them with what was in him. Hence, they always believed he meant his words.

So his heart was always growing—and where the heart grows, there the intellect also grows. He was a very good father to his people, and not foolishly kind. He tried his best to help them to be what they ought to be, to make them bear their troubles, be true to one another, and govern themselves. Perhaps it was because he was so good to his flock that God gave him little Clare to bring up. Perhaps it was because he and his wife were so good to Clare that, by and by, a wonderful thing took place.

About three years after the earthquake, Mrs. Porson had a baby girl sent her for her very own. The father and mother thought themselves the happiest couple on the face of the earth—and who knows but they were!

When Clare first saw his baby sister Mary, he looked down on her with solemn, unmoved countenance, and gazed changeless for a whole minute. He thought there had been another earthquake, that another church dome had fallen, and another child been found and brought home from the ruin. Then light began to grow somewhere under his face. The light grew till his face was radiant, and then out of the midst of the shining broke a heavenly smile. After this he smiled occasionally, though still seldom. A quiet peace, like the stillness of a long summer twilight in the north, dwelt upon his visage. Part of his life seemed away, and he waiting for it to come back. Then he would be merry!

He never was in a hurry, yet always doing something—always, that is, when he was not in his own room. There his mother would sometimes find him sitting absolutely still, with his hands on his knees. Nor was she sorry to surprise him thus, for then she was sure of one of his rare smiles. She thought he must then be dreaming of his own mother, and a pang would go through her at the thought that he would one day love her more than herself. "He will laugh then!" she said. She did not think how the gratitude of that mother would one day overwhelm *her* with gladness.

Clare never sought to be cuddled, but always snuggled to one that drew him close. He learned what lessons were set him—not very fast, but with persistent endeavor to understand. He was greatly given to reading, but not particularly quick.

When first he was allowed to take little Mary in his arms, it was almost a new start in his existence. A new confidence was born in his spirit. Mrs. Porson could read, as if reflected in his countenance, the pride and tenderness that composed so much of her own conscious motherhood. A certain staidness took possession of Clare's face as he bent over the helpless creature, half on his knees, half in his arms—the sternness of a protecting divinity that knew danger was not far off.

He had taken a step upward in being: he was aware in himself, without knowing it, of the dignity of fatherhood. Even now he knew what so many seem never to learn, that a man is the defender of the weak—that, if a man is his brother's keeper, still more is he his sister's. Mary belonged to him, therefore he was hers in the slavery of love, which alone is freedom. So reverential and so careful did he show himself, that soon his mother trusted him, to the extent of his power, more than any nurse.

And yet she was disturbed when she first heard what he murmured to the baby, half singing and half talking:

"Baby, baby, do not grow," he said. "Keep small, and lie on my lap, and dream of walking, but never walk; for when you walk, you will run, and when you run, you will go away with Father and Mother—away to a big place where the ground goes up to the sky, and you will come into a big church, and the ground and the church and the sky will go *hurr, hurr, hurr;* and the sky, full of angels, will come down with a great roar out of the sky, and tumble down Father and Mother, and hold them down so they cannot get up again; and then you will have nobody but me. I will do all I can, but I am only brother Clare, and you will want Mother and Father, and they will be always coming, and never come, not for ever so long! Don't grow a big girl, Mary!"

The mother could not think what to say. She went in and, in the hope of turning his thoughts aside, took the baby, and made haste to consult her husband.

"We must leave it," said Mr. Porson. "Experience will soon correct what mistake is in his notion. It is not so very far wrong. You and I must go from them one day: what is it but that the sky will fall down on us, and our bodies will get up no more! He thinks the time nearer at hand than for their sakes I hope it is—but nobody can tell."

Clare never associated the church where the awful thing took place with the church to which he went on Sundays. The time for it, he imagined, came to everybody. The way out of the world was a church in a city set on a hill, and there an earthquake was always ready.

CHAPTER THREE
Clare and His Brothers

After a year or two, Mr. Porson became anxious that Clare should grow up to be too unmanly. He began, therefore, to take him with him about the parish, and was delighted to find he had extraordinary endurance. Clare could walk many miles and come home again less tired than his father. He continued slight and thin, but the muscles of his little bird-like legs seemed of steel.

One day Mr. Porson was calling at Mr. Goodenough's farm near the parsonage. The farmer's wife was ill, and having to go to her room to see her, he said to the boy, "Clare, you run into the yard. Give my compliments to anyone you meet, and ask him to let you stay with him."

When the time came for them to leave, Mr. Porson went to find the boy. He had not to call twice: out of the covered part of the pigsty Clare came creeping on all fours, followed by a litter of half-grown, grunting, gamboling pigs.

"Here I am, Papa!" he cried.

"Clare!" exclaimed his father. "What a mess you have made of yourself!"

"I gave them your compliments," answered the boy, as he scrambled over the fence, "and asked them if I might stay with them till you were ready. They said yes, and invited me in. I went in, and we've been having such games! They were very kind to me."

His father looked into the sty. There stood all the pigs in a row, gazing after the boy, and looking as sorry as their thick skins and bony snouts would let them. Their mother rose in a ridge behind them, gazing too.

If Clare's love of the animals began with the pigs, it was far from ending with them. The next day Clare asked if he might go and call upon the pigs.

"Have you forgotten, Clare," said his mother, "what a job Susan and I had with your clothes? I wonder still how you could have done such a thing! When I saw you, I had half a mind to put you in a bath, clothes and all. I doubt if they are clean yet!"

"Oh, yes, they are, indeed, Mamma!" returned Clare. "And you know I shall be careful after this! I shall not go into their sty, but get the farmer to let them out. I've thought of a new game with them!"

His mother consented. The farmer did let the pigs out, and Clare and they had a right good game together in the yard.

His growing nature showed itself in a swiftly widening friendship for live things—the cows and the horses, the hens and the geese, and every creature about the place. He called the pigs little brothers, and the horses and cows his big brothers, and was perfectly at home with them before people knew he cared for their company.

There was one dangerous animal on the place—Nimrod, a bull, of which Farmer Goodenough had often said he must part with him, or he would be the death of somebody. One morning Farmer Goodenough was struck with terror to find Clare in Nimrod's stall. The brute was chained up pretty short, but was free enough for terrible mischief. Clare was stroking his nose, and the beast was standing as still as a bull of bronze, with one forward-curved, wicked horn alarmingly close to Clare's angelic face.

The farmer called Clare, and the boy came at once. Mr. Goodenough told him he must not go near Nimrod, for the bull was fierce and dangerous. Clare replied that he and the bull had been friends for a long time—and to prove it, ran back and perched on the animal's shoulders. The bull went on eating the grass in the manger before him, and took no notice of the boy.

Everyone in the parish knew the boy and his story. From his gentleness and loving-kindness to live things, there were some who said he was half-witted; others said he saw ghosts. The boys of the village hated him because he was so unlike them.

The days are long in boyhood, and Clare could do many things in one day. He could help on the farm; he could play with ever so many animals; he could learn his lessons, which happily were not heavy; he could read any book he pleased in his father's library, where *Paradise Lost* was his favorite; and he could tend little "Maly," which was what he called her. He had more time for all these since he had no companion of his own age, no one he wanted to go about with after school hours. His father was still his chief human companion, and neither of them grew tired of the other.

Clare was too busy loving, with so many about him to love, to think about being loved himself. And the animals, though they were not aware of it, did much to save him from being spoiled by the humans whom the boy loved more than them. For Clare's charity began at home.

One incident with an animal befell Clare and caused him a sore heart, making him feel like a traitor to the whole animal race, and influencing his life forever.

He had seen men go out shooting, but had never himself used a gun. He was at the bottom of the garden one afternoon with the stick of a worn-out umbrella in his hand. Suddenly a half-grown rabbit rose in the grass before him and bolted. In imitation of the hunters, Clare raised the stick to his shoulder, and said *Bang!* The rabbit gave a great bound into the air, fell, and lay motionless. Clare approached the rabbit, trembling.

"I dare say the little one knows me," he said to himself, "and wanted to give me a start!"

When he drew near, however, "the little one" did not jump up and run again. With sinking heart Clare went close up, and looked down on it. The rabbit lay stretched out, motionless. With death in his own heart, Clare stooped and lifted it, pressed it tenderly to his heart, and went with it to find his mother. The tears kept pouring down his face, but he uttered no cry till he came to her. Then a low groaning howl burst from him; he laid the dead thing in her lap, and threw himself on the floor at her feet.

She asked him if he had found it dead. He only shook his head, but that head-shake had a whole tragedy in it. Then she examined "the little one," but could find no mark or wound on it. When she learned what had happened, she tried to comfort Clare, insisting he was not to blame, for he did not mean to kill the little one, and that it had probably died of a weak heart.

"No, Mother!" he said through his sobs. "I wouldn't have blamed myself if I had killed him by accident—but I *meant* to frighten him! I made him think I was an enemy, and going to kill him!" He stopped with a most wailful howl.

"I ought to have thought, Mother, of what I was doing. I was trying to frighten him. To think that I pulled down the roof of his church upon him!"

Clare burst into a torrent of tears, and ran to his own room. By the time his mother called him to tea, calmness had taken the place of the agony on his countenance. The boy had reflected that things could not go so wrong that nobody could set them right; if he had done the rabbit a wrong, as he never for a moment to the end of his life doubted he had, He who is at the head of all heads and the heart of all hearts, would contrive to let him tell the rabbit he was sorry, and would give him something to do for the rabbit that would make up for his cruelty to him.

One cold day in a stormy March, the wind was wildly blowing broken clouds across the heavens, and now rain, now sleet, over the shivering blades of the young corn. Clare was hovering about the plow when he suddenly spied a little procession passing along the road. Six people in front carried a heavy coffin on their shoulders, and behind it one man walked alone.

For a moment Clare watched him, and saw his bowed

head and heavy pace. His heart filled from its own perennial fount of pity, which was God Himself in him. He ran down the hill and across the next field, making for a spot some distance ahead of the procession. As it passed him, he joined the chief mourner, who went plodding on with his arms hanging by his sides. Creeping close up to him, he slid his little soft hand into the great calloused hand of the peasant. Instinctively, the big hand closed upon the small one, and the weather-beaten face of a man of fifty looked down on the boy. Not a word was said between them as they walked on, hand in hand.

Neither had ever seen the other. The man was following his wife and his one child to the grave.

Clare, without knowing it, had taken the man under the protection of his love—and now went with him to the grave, joined in the service, and saw the grave filled. They went again as they had come, without a word being spoken. The man wept a little now and then, drew the back of his brown hand across his eyes, and pressed a little closer the hand he held. At the gate of the parsonage, the boy took his leave. He said they would be wondering what had become of him, or he would have gone farther. The man released him without a word.

His mother had been uneasy about him, but when he tóld her how it was, she said he had done right.

"Yes," returned the boy. "I belong there myself."

The mother knew he was not thinking of the grave. He was so unlike most boys that one must know all about him to understand him.

CHAPTER FOUR
Clare the Defender

Never yet had the boy shown any anger. His father was a little troubled by this, fearing such an absence of resentment might indicate moral indifference, or might leave him unable to cope with the world.

One day a coarse village boy—Simpson—gave Clare a sharp blow on the face, forcing water from his eyes and blood from his nose. Clare was wiping away at both at once with his handkerchief when a kindly girl stopped and said to him, "Never mind—don't cry."

"Oh, no!" answered Clare. "It's only water; it's not crying. It would be cowardly to cry."

"That's a brave boy! You'll give it back one of these days."

"No," he returned, "I shall not. I couldn't."

"Why?"

"Because it hurts so."

The girl, as well as the boys who stood around him, burst into laughter. They saw no logic in his reasoning. Clare's was the divine reasoning that comes of loving your neighbor; theirs was the earthly reasoning that came of loving themselves.

This same boy Simpson troubled every decent person in the neighborhood. It was well his mother was a widow, for where she was only powerless to restrain, the father would have encouraged. He was a big, idle, sneering, insolent lad— had there been two more of the sort, they would have made the village uninhabitable.

One day, when little Mary was about five years old, Clare had her out for a walk. They were alone in a narrow lane, next to the Goodenough farm. Down the lane to meet them came Simpson. He strolled up with his hands in his pockets, and barred their way. Mary slipped past him, and the young brute darted after the child. Clare put down his head, as the rams do, and as Simpson was on the point of laying hold of her, caught him in the flank, butted him into the ditch, and fell on top of him.

"Run, Maly!" he cried. "I'll be after you in a moment."

"Will you, you little devil!" cried the bully, and taking him by the throat, so that he could not utter even a gurgle, got up and began to beat him unmercifully. But the sound of their conflict had reached the ears of the bull Nimrod, who was feeding within the hedge. He recognized Clare's voice, and perhaps knew from it that he was in trouble. He came tearing to the scene, looked over the hedge, and saw his friend in the clutches of an enemy of his own, for Simpson never lost a chance of teasing Nimrod when he could do so with safety.

Over Nimrod came with a short roar and a crash. Looking up, the bully saw a bigger bully than himself, with his head down and his horns level, retreating a step or two in preparation for running at him. Simpson shoved the helpless Clare toward the enemy and fled. Clare fell, but Nimrod jumped over his prostrate friend and tore after Simpson. Clare got up and would at once have followed to protect his enemy, but first he must see his sister safe. He left her at the next cottage and returned to pursue Simpson and the bull.

Nimrod overtook Simpson in the act of scrambling over a five-barred gate. CRASH! Against the gate came Nimrod's horns, with all the weight and speed of his body behind them. Away went the gate into the field, and away went Simpson and the bull with it. His horns were entangled in the bars, and Simpson's right leg was jammed between the gate and the head and the horns of the bull. Simpson roared, and his roars maddened Nimrod, furious already that he could not get his horns clear.

Clare had not seen the catastrophe, and did not know

what had become of the pursuer or pursued until he reached the gap where the gate had been. Then he saw the odd struggle going on, and ran to the aid of his foe, in terror of what might already have befallen him. The moment he laid hold of one of the animal's horns, the infuriated Nimrod quieted, and yielded to the small hands as they pushed and pulled his head this way and that until they got it clear of the gate. But then the hands did not let him go. Clare proceeded to take him home, and Nimrod made no objection. Simpson lay groaning.

When Clare returned, his enemy was still there. He had got clear of the gate, but seemed in much pain, for he lay tearing up the grass and sod in handfuls. When Clare stooped to ask what he should do for him, Simpson struck him a backhanded blow on the face that knocked him over. Clare got up and ran.

"Coward!" cried Simpson. "Leaving a man with a broken leg to get home by himself!"

"I'm going to find someone strong enough to help you," said Clare.

But Simpson, after his own evil nature, imagined Clare was going to let the bull into the field again, and fell to praying him not to leave. But Clare made haste to tell the people at the farm, and Simpson lay in terror of the bull till help came.

From that hour Simpson hated Clare, attributing to him all the ill he had brought on himself. But he was out of mischief for a while. As a result of the incident, the bully was crippled for life, and could do the less harm.

It was a great joy to Mr. Porson to learn how Clare had defended Mary against Simpson.

"Weren't you afraid of such a big rascal?" Mr. Porson asked.

"No, Papa," answered the boy. "Should I have been?" He put his hand to his forehead, as if trying to understand, and his father found he had himself something to think about.

CHAPTER FIVE

A Dark Summer

When Clare was ten a peculiar form of fever, though not usually fatal, greatly affected many in the village. From morning to night the parson and his wife helped the cottagers, depriving themselves of a good part of their own food and warmth. When at last the parson's strength gave way and the fever laid hold of him, he had to do without many comforts his wife would gladly have gotten for him. They were both from humble beginnings, but Mrs. Porson did have one well-to-do relative, a sister who had married a rich but very common man. From her they could not ask any help. She had never sent them anything, and had been fiercely indignant with them for adopting Clare.

Neither of the Porsons once complained, though Mrs. Porson, whose strength was much spent, could not help weeping sometimes when she was alone. They knew their Lord did not live in luxury, and a secret gladness nestled in their hearts that they were allowed to suffer a little with Him.

But John Porson's hour was come. He died, leaving his wife, children, and parish, to go to meet his Lord. Mrs. Porson wept, but before she had time to wonder how she was to live and rear her children, she too died.

Clare was in the garden when Susan, the housekeeper, told him his mother was dead. He stood still for a moment, then looked up, up into the sky. Two slow tears gathered, rolled over, and dried upon his face. He turned to Mary, lifted her in his arms, carried her about the garden, and once more told her his strange version of what had happened in his childhood. Then he told her that her papa and mamma had gone to look for his papa and mamma—"somewhere up in the dome," he said.

One cold noon not long after, Clare and Mary sat by the kitchen fire. Susan was cooking their midday meal, which had come from her own pocket. She was the only servant either of them had known in the house, and she would not leave it until someone should take charge of them.

With a sudden jingle and rattle, up drove a rickety carriage to the door of the parsonage. Out of it, and into the kitchen, came stalking a stern-faced middle-age woman in a long black cloak, black bonnet, and black gloves.

"I am the late Mrs. Porson's sister," she said.

Susan curtsied and waited. Clare rose, with Mary in his arms. "This is little Maly, ma'am," he said.

Mary put her finger in her mouth, and began to cry.

"Tut! Tut!" said the aunt. "Crying already! That will never do if you are going to live with me! Show me her things."

Susan felt stunned. She sent quietly for the aid of Farmer Goodenough, but Mary's few things were soon packed, and she was carried off, shrieking, struggling, and calling for "Clay." The aunt, however, cared nothing for Mary's protests. Clare was seized and held back by Farmer Goodenough.

The carriage was not yet out of sight when Farmer Goodenough began to regret that he had come: his presence was an acknowledgment of responsibility! Something had to be done with the foundling! There was nobody to claim Clare, and nobody wanted him. Mr. Goodenough had always liked the boy, but he did not want him. His wife was not fond of the boy—or any boy—and did not want him.

"Where are *you* going?" he asked Susan. "We can't have you on the parish, you know!"

"I beg your pardon, sir, but until the child here is provided for, or until they turn us out of the parsonage, I will not leave the place."

"The furniture is advertised for sale. You'll have nothing but bare walls!"

"We'll manage to keep each other warm."

"Won't you ask Mr. Goodenough to stay for dinner?" Clare said. He went up to the farmer and laid his arm against his.

"He would eat all we have," answered Susan, "and not have enough!"

"Now Maly is gone," returned Clare, "I would rather not have any dinner."

The farmer's old feeling for the boy came back. "Get him his dinner, Susan," he said. "I've something to see to in the village. By the time I come back, he'll be ready to go with me perhaps."

"God bless you, sir!" cried Susan. "You meant it all the time, an' I been behavin' like a brute!"

The farmer had promised nothing, but he had nearly made up his mind that, as the friend of the late parson, he could scarcely do less than give shelter to the child until he found another refuge. There were many things Clare could do around the farm to make himself useful.

When Mr. Goodenough appeared at home with the boy, his wife's face expressed what her tongue dared not utter. But Clare never saw that he was unwelcome.

True to her nature, Mrs. Goodenough made Clare pay for his keep. Occasionally he attended the village school, where the old master was doing his best for him. But usually Mrs. Goodenough prevented his going, and gave him chores to do around the house, the dairy, and the poultry yard. His acquaintance with the poultry and the pigs, the pigeons and the calves, especially the animals that had been hurt, rapidly increased.

Clare now came more into contact with the larger animals around the farm, and derived great comfort from them. He was still friendly with Nimrod, the bull, and the people around the farm frequently sought Clare's help with the animal, for at times they dared hardly approach him.

But Clare's main interest lay in the horses. When he was alone with them, he talked to them about the friends he had lost—his father and mother and Mary and Susan. He would even tell them sometimes about his own father and mother—how the sky full of angels fell down upon them and took them away. But he talked most about his sister, for he mourned her more than any of the rest. Mary had always needed *him,* and more than ever in the last days of their companionship. He wept for nobody but Mary. In the night he would wake up suddenly, thinking he heard her crying out for him. Then he would get out of bed, creep to the stable, go to his favorite horse Jonathan, and to him pour out his low-voiced complaint.

In the village, some began to remark that Clare no longer looked "the little gentleman." His clothes were not fit for the work he was doing, and within a few weeks were very shabby. Besides, he was growing rapidly, so that he and his garments were too evidently parting company. Accustomed to a mother's attentions, Clare had never thought of his clothes except to take care of them for her sake. Now he tried to mend them, but soon found his labor of little use. He had no money to buy anything with, and his clothes or his health or his education were nothing to Mrs. Goodenough.

When the winter came, Clare's sufferings must at times have been considerable. In the day his work was a protection, but at night the house was cold. He had, however, plenty to eat, had no ailment, and was not to be greatly pitied.

Some of his old troubles were not yet over. Simpson the bully went limping about on a crutch, permanently lame and full of hatred toward Clare for the injury he had brought upon himself. Ever since his recovery, Simpson had loitered about, waiting to catch him off guard. Not until Clare went to the farm, however, did Simpson succeed.

Clare went home bleeding and torn. The righteous churchwarden rebuked him with severity for fighting, and Mrs. Goodenough told Clare she was glad he had met with someone to give him what he deserved. He stared at her with wondering eyes, but said nothing. She turned from them: the devil in her could not look in the eyes of the angel in him. The next time he fell into Simpson's snare, he managed to hide what had befallen him. After that he was too wide-awake to be caught.

There was in the village a boy who had no family. Tommy was far more destitute than Clare, but had too much liberty. He lived with a wretched old woman who called him her grandson; whether he was or not nobody cared. She made her living by renting beds in her cottage to travellers and tramps. Tommy was thus thrown into the worst of company, and learned many sorts of wickedness.

Small and deft, Tommy was already a thief and pickpocket, but he had never gone to jail. He was a miserable creature, barefooted and bare-legged, about eight years of age, but so stunted that he looked less than six. He had keen ferret eyes in red rims, red hair, a freckled face, and a generally unhealthy look.

Tommy first met Clare when Clare rescued him from a severe beating being administered by his grandmother. A friendship, for long almost a silent one, was thus initiated between them.

By and by this friendship came to Simpson's knowledge. One day Simpson saw Clare coming, and Tommy waiting for him. He laid hold of Tommy, and began cuffing him and pulling his hair to make him scream, thinking thus to get hold of Clare. But Clare flew to the rescue, caught up the crutch Simpson had dropped, and whacked it across his back with vigor. The fellow let Tommy go and turned on Clare, who went backward, brandishing the crutch.

"Run, Tommy!" Clare cried.

Tommy retreated a few steps. "Run yourself," he counseled. "Take his third leg with you."

Clare saw the advice was good and ran. But he turned, and saw his enemy hobbling after him in evident pain and discomfort. Clare went to meet him, and politely gave him his crutch. Then Simpson laid him flat on the ground with one swing of the crutch, and began to beat him.

Tommy stood and watched. "Clare's older an' bigger an' pluckier than me," he said to himself, "but he's a fool. He'll come to grief unless he's looked after. He don't know how to dodge. I'll have to take him in charge!" When he saw Clare free, Tommy turned and ran home.

Simpson redoubled his persecution of Clare, and also persecuted Tommy because of Clare. He lurked for Tommy now, and tormented him, and made his life miserable. After every encounter, Tommy would hurry to see Clare.

Hot tears would come to Clare's eyes as he listened to the not-always-unembellished tale of Tommy's sufferings at the hands of Simpson. But Clare never thought of revenge, only of protection or escape for the boy. It comforted him to believe that he was growing, and would soon be a match for Simpson.

But the hour arrived when Mrs. Goodenough could bear Clare's presence no longer. Some petty loss had befallen her, and nothing touched her like the loss of money. She opened the sluices of her hate, and overwhelmed Clare with it in the presence of her husband.

Farmer Goodenough knew she was unfair, knew Clare was a good and diligent boy, and knew there was nothing against him but the hatred of his wife. But, annoyed with her injustice, he was powerless to change her heart. Before Clare had come to live with them, the farmer had had no pleasure in his wife's company. She had always been moody and dissatisfied; but since Clare's arrival she had been unbearable. Constantly irritated with and by her because of Clare, Mr. Goodenough had begun to regard Clare as the destroyer of his peace, and to feel a grudge against him. He sat smoldering with bodiless rage, and said nothing.

Clare too was silent—for what could he say? Where is the wisdom that can answer hatred? He carried to his friend Jonathan a heavy and perplexed heart.

"Why does she hate me so, Jonathan?" Clare murmured.

The big horse kissed his head all over, but made him no other answer.

CHAPTER SIX

The Vagabonds

The next morning Clare did something not to the farmer's liking. The boy cleaned that side of one of the cow houses first which was usually cleaned last. Mr. Goodenough gave him a box on the ear that made Clare stagger, and then stand bewildered.

"What do you mean by staring that way?" cried the farmer. "Am I not to box your ears when I choose?" And with that he struck the boy again.

Then it dawned on Clare that he was not wanted. He threw down his scraper, and ran from the cow house through the farm to the lane, and from the lane to the road.

At the mouth of the lane, where it opened on the road, Clare ran into Tommy turning the corner, eager to find him. Tommy's eyes were swollen with weeping; his nose was bleeding, and scarcely recognizable as a nose. The protector awoke in Clare, and he stopped, unable to speak, but not unable to listen. Tommy blubbered out a confused, half-inarticulate something about "Granny and the other devil," who between them had all but killed him.

"What can I do?" Clare said, his heart sinking with the sense of not being able to help.

Tommy was ready to answer the question, for he had been hatching vengeance all the way. He eagerly proposed that they should wait in ambush for Simpson, and knock his crutch out from under him. That done, Clare should beat him with it, while Tommy ran like the wind and set his grandmother's house on fire.

"She'll be drunk in bed, an' she'll be burned to death!"

cried Tommy. "Then we'll mizzle!"*

"But it would hurt them both very badly, Tommy!" said Clare, as if unfolding the reality of the thing to a foolish child.

"Well, all right! The worse the better! Ain't they hurt *us?*" rejoined Tommy.

"That's how we know it's not nice!" answered Clare. "If they started it, we ain't to keep it a-going!"

"Then they'll be at it forever," cried Tommy, "an' I'm sick of it! I'll *kill* Granny! I swear I will, if I'm hanged for it! She's said a hundred times she'd pull my legs when I was hanged—but *she* won't be at the hanging!"

"Why don't you run for it first?" Clare asked. "Then they wouldn't want to hang you."

"Then I wouldn't have nobody!" replied Tommy, whimpering.

"I should have thought Nobody was as good as Granny!" said Clare.

"I wasn't meanin' Granny—nor yet stumpin' Simpson," Tommy answered.

"I don't know what you're driving at," Clare said.

Tommy burst into tears. "Ain't you the only one I got, Clare?" he cried.

"Well," rejoined Clare, struggling with his misery, "ain't I going myself?"

"What! You're leaving Farmer Goodenough? Won't he be sad?"

"He'll think himself well rid of me," returned Clare with a sigh. "But there's no time to talk. If you're going, Tommy, come along." Clare turned to go.

"Where to?" asked Tommy, following.

"I don't know. Anywhere away," answered Clare, quickening his pace.

In spite of his swollen face, Tommy's eyes grew wider. "You ain't stole nothin'?"

Clare stopped, and for the first time on his own part, lifted his hand to strike. It dropped immediately by his side. "No,

Tommy," he said. "I don't steal."

"What are you running away for then?"

"Because they don't want me."

"What will you do?"

"Work."

Tommy held his tongue; he knew a better way than that! If work was the only road to eating, things would go badly with *him!* He would go with Clare, but not to work!

*****

It was a lovely spring morning. The boys walked more than a mile before they came to a pond by a farmhouse. Clare had been observing with pity how wretched Tommy's clothes were, but when he looked into the pond he saw that his own shabbiness was worse than Tommy's. What he wore had once been his Sunday suit, but now it was not even worth brushing!

"I'm 'orrid 'ungry," said Tommy. "I ain't swallered a plug this mornin', 'xcep' a lump o' bread out o' Granny's cupboard. That's what I got my weltin' for. It were a whole half-loaf, though—an' none so dry!"

Clare had eaten nothing, and had been up since five o'clock—at work all the time till the farmer struck him. He was quite as hungry as Tommy, but what was to be done? Besides a pocket-handkerchief, he had but one thing worth bartering.*

The very day she was taken ill, Clare had been in the storeroom with Mrs. Porson, and she, knowing the pleasure he took in the scent of brown Windsor soap, had given him a small cake. This he had kept in his pocket ever since, wrapped in a piece of rose-colored paper, his one cherished possession. Yet, with hunger deadening his sorrow, the time had come to bid it farewell.

Clare and Tommy went to the door of the farmhouse and knocked. It was opened by a matron who looked at them over the horizon of her chin.

"Please, ma'am," said Clare, "will you give us a piece of bread? As large a piece, please, as you can spare, and I will give you this piece of brown Windsor soap." As he ended his speech, he took a farewell whiff of his favorite.

"Soap!" retorted the dame. "Who wants your soap? Where did you get it? Stole it, I don't doubt!" She took it in her hand and held it to her nose. "Who gave it to you?"

"My mother," answered Clare.

"Where's your mother?"

Clare pointed upward.

"Eh? Oh, hanged! I *thought* so!" She threw the soap into the yard and closed the door. Clare darted after his property, pounced upon it, and restored it lovingly to his pocket.

As the boys were leaving the yard, they saw a cart full of turnips. Tommy turned and flew at the cart, but Clare caught and held him, crying, "Don't, Tommy! They ain't ours!"

"Why not? I'm hungry," answered Tommy, "an' you see it's no use astin'!"

"To take it wouldn't make it ours, Tommy."

"Wouldn't it, though? When I'd eaten it, it would be mine!"

"No, it wouldn't. Think of having in your stomach what wasn't yours! No, you must pay for it. Perhaps they would take my soap for a turnip. I believe it's worth two turnips."

Clare spied a man under a shed, ran to him, and offered him the soap for a turnip apiece.

"I don't want your soap," the man answered, "an' I don't recommend cold turmits of a mornin'. But take one if you like, and clear out."

"Ain't you the master, sir?"

"No, I ain't."

"Then the turnips ain't yours?" Clare asked, looking at him with hungry, regretful eyes.

"You're a deal too impudent to be hungry!" said the man. "Be off with you, or I'll set the dog on you."

"I'm very sorry," Clare said. "I did not mean to offend you."

"Clear out, I say. Double trot!"

Hungry as the boys were, they left with no bread and no

turnips.

About five miles further, they sat down on the roadside where Tommy began to cry. Clare did not try to stop him. By and by a workingman came along the road and stopped. He questioned Clare and listened to his story, then counseled the boys to go back home.

"I'm not wanted, sir," said Clare.

"They'd kill *me*," said Tommy.

"God help you, boys!" the man answered. "You may be telling me lies, and you may be telling me the truth. A liar may be hungry, but somehow I grudge my dinner to a liar!"

As he spoke, he untied his dinner from its blue handkerchief and gave them its contents of bread and cheese. Then he wiped his face with the cloth, put it in his pocket, lifted his bag of tools, and went his way.

The dinner went a good way toward satisfying the boys. They started again refreshed and hopeful.

As the evening drew on into night, a new worry arose in Clare's mind. How would they find shelter for sleep? It was a question that gave Tommy no anxiety, for he had been on the tramp often, and had frequently slept in the open air or under the rudest cover.

But to inexperienced Clare, there was something fearful in having the night come so close to him. To lie down with the stars looking at him, and nothing but the blue wind between him and them, was like being naked to the very soul. Doubtless there would be creatures about to share the night with him, and protect him from its awful bareness—but they would be few for the size of the room, and he might see none of them! It was the sense of emptiness, the lack of present life that dismayed him. He had never seen any creatures to shrink from. He disliked no one of the things that creep or fly. It was Nothing that he feared.

He had heard a great deal about God, and about Jesus Christ, but They always seemed persons a long way off. He knew, or thought he knew, that God was everywhere, but he had never felt His presence a reality. He never thought, "God is here." When he looked out into the night it always seemed vacant, therefore horrid, and he took it for as empty as it looked. And if there had been no God there, it would have been reasonable indeed to be afraid; for the most frightful of notions is *Nothing-at-all.*

It grew dark, and the boys were falling asleep on their walking legs, when they came to a barnyard. Searching for the warmest place, they crawled into the stable. Tommy, who was afraid of the horses, stayed close to Clare. Clare's hand fell upon the hindquarters of a large horse, and at the touch of the small hand it gave a low whinny. Tommy shuddered at the sound.

"He's pleased," Clare said, and crept up on his near side into the stall. There he made friends with the horse, and got in among the hay the horse had for his supper. The animal's great nostrils snuffed over him as he lay, and made him welcome. Clare went to sleep stroking the muzzle of the horse and slept all night, kept warm by the horse's breath and the near furnace of his great body.

Tommy coiled himself up in an empty stall and was soon fast asleep.

The next morning the boys slept too long and were discovered. But though they were promptly ejected as vagabonds, and with a few kicks and cuffs, these were not administered without the restraint of some mercy, for the boys' appearance tended to draw pity rather than anger.

CHAPTER SEVEN
On the Tramp

With the new day came the fresh necessity for breakfast, and the fresh interest in finding it. Passing the half-open door of a flour mill, Clare and Tommy saw a heap of dusty flour sweepings. They swallowed a considerable portion of the flour, choking as it was—but there was good food in it, and they might have fared worse.

Another day's tramp was thus begun. How it was to end no one in the world knew less than the trampers.

Clare had lived with much the same feeling with which he read a story: he was in the story, half dreaming, half acting it. He was a dreamer with open eyes and ready hands, not clearly distinguishing thought from action, fancy from fact.

Yet Clare was in the process of being changed from a dreamer to a man. Clare began to see that everybody in the world has to do something in order to get food—he had worked for the farmer and his wife, and they had fed him. He had worked willingly and eaten gladly, but had not before put the two together. He saw now that men who would be men must work.

Clare had read stories about thieves and honest boys, but he did not know how difficult it is not to be a thief—that is, to be downright honest. He began to see that it is not enough to mean well; that he must be sharp, and mind what he was about, or else, with hunger worrying inside him, he might be a thief before he knew. Clare was finding out that to *think* rightly—to be on the side of what is honorable—is a very different thing from *doing* right, and *being* honorable, when the temptation is upon us.

The mill sweepings did not last the boys long, and by the time they saw the spires and chimneys of a small town, they were very hungry indeed. Clare wondered how he would get work: Tommy was too small to do anything, so Clare would have to earn enough for both of them. He could think of nothing but going into shops, or knocking at the house doors, and asking for something to do. He never thought how much his outward appearance was working against him, or how unwilling anyone would be to hire him, or what a disadvantage the company of Tommy was, because he had every mark of a born thief.

Suddenly Tommy ran from his side, unseen by Clare, who became again aware of him by finding himself pulled toward the entrance of a narrow lane. Clare yielded, and went with him into the lane, but stopped immediately. For he saw that Tommy had under his arm a big loaf, and the steam of newly baked bread was fragrant in his nostrils.

"Where did you get that beautiful loaf, Tommy?" he asked.

"Off a baker's cart," said Tommy. "Don't be skeered—he never saw me!"

"Then you stole it?"

"Yes," grumbled Tommy, "if that's the name you put upon it when your trousers is so slack you've got to hold on to them or they'd trip you up!"

"Where's the cart?"

"In the street there."

"Come along."

Clare took the loaf from Tommy, and turned to find the baker's cart. They had scarcely turned the corner when they came upon it. The baker was looking the other way, so Clare decided to lay down the loaf and walk away. But in the very act the baker turned, saw Clare, and sprang upon him.

"I have you!" he cried, and shook Clare as if he would have shaken his head off.

"It's quite a mistake, sir!" was all Clare could get out.

"Mistaken, am I? I like that! Police!" And with that, the baker shook him again.

A policeman heard the man call, and came running.

"Here's a gen'leman as wants the honor o' your acquaintance!" said the baker.

But Tommy saw that he was more likely to get off than Clare if he told the truth. "Please, policeman," he said, "it wasn't *him*—it was me who took the loaf."

"You little liar!" the baker shouted. "Didn't I see him with his hand on the loaf?"

"He was puttin' it back," said Tommy. "If he'd only ha' let me run, there wouldn't ha' been nobody the wiser. I *am* sorry I didn't run. Oh, I *ham* so 'ungry!" Tommy doubled himself up around his hands.

"'Ungry, are you?" roared the baker. "That's what thieves off a baker's cart *ought* to be! 'Ungry to all eternity!"

"Look here!" cried a pale-faced mechanic in front of the gathering crowd. "There's a way of telling whether the boy's speakin' the truth *now!*" He caught up the restored loaf, halved it, and handed each of the boys a part. The boys tore at the delicious bread, blind and deaf to all about them.

"Now, baker, what's the cost?" the mechanic asked.

"Sixpence," said the man sullenly.

The mechanic laid sixpence on the cover of the cart. "I ought to ha' made you weigh and make up," he said. "Where's your scales?"

"Mind to your own business." The baker moved off with his cart, and the crowd began to disperse.

The boys stood absorbed, each in what remained of his half-loaf. When he looked up, Clare saw that they were alone. But he saw the mechanic some way off, and ran after him. "Oh, sir!" he said, "I was so hungry, I didn't thank you for the loaf. We'd had nothing today but the sweepings of a mill."

"God bless my soul!" said the man. "People say there's a God!" he added.

"I think there must be, sir, for you came by just then!" returned Clare.

"How do you come to be so hard up, my boy? Somebody's to blame somewhere!"

"There ain't no harm in being hungry, so long as the loaf comes!" rejoined Clare. "When I get work we will be all right!"

"That's your sort!" said the man. "But if there had been a God, as people say, He would ha' made me fit to gi'e you a job, i'stead o' stan'in' here with ne'er a turn o' work to do for myself."

"I'll work my hardest to pay you back your sixpence," said Clare.

"No, no, don't you worry about that. I ha' got two or three more i' my pocket, thank God!"

"You have two Gods, then, sir?" said Clare. "One who does things for you, and one who don't?"

"Come, you young shaver—you're too much for me!" laughed the man.

Tommy came shyly up, looking impudent now he was filled, with his hands where his pockets should have been.

"It was you who stole the loaf, you little rascal!" said the workman, seeing *thief* in every line of the boy.

"Yes," answered Tommy boldly, "an' I don't see no harm. The baker had lots, and he wasn't 'ungry. It was Clare who made a mess of it! He deserved what he got! The loaf was mine—*I* stole it!"

"Oh, ho! It wasn't his! It was yours, was it! Why do you run about with a chap like this, young gentleman?" asked the man, turning to Clare. "I know you ain't been brought up alongside o' him!"

"I had to go away, and he came with me," answered Clare.

"You'd better get rid of him. He'll get you into trouble."

"I can't get rid of him," Clare replied. "But I will teach him not to take what isn't his. He don't know better. He's been ill-used all his life."

"You don't seem over well-used yourself," said the man.

He saw that Clare's clothes had been made for a boy in good circumstances, though they were worn and grimy.

"Look here, young master," he continued. "You have no right to be in company with that boy. He'll bring you grief, and be the loss of your character."

"I ain't got a character to lose," replied Clare. "I thought I had, but when nobody will believe me, where's my character then?"

"Now you're wrong there," returned the man. "*I* believe every word you say, and should be very sorry to find myself mistaken."

"Thank you, sir," said Clare. "May I carry your bag for you?"

"I guess I'm the abler-bodied pauper!" answered the man. Picking up his bag, he walked away.

"Tommy!" Clare said in a tone new to himself, for a new sense of moral protection had risen in him. "If *ever* you steal anything again, either I'll give you a hiding,* or you and I will part company."

Tommy bored his knuckles into his red eyes and began to whimper. He had looked to Clare to supply the strength and the innocent look, while he supplied the head and the lively fingers—and here was Clare knocking the lovely plan to pieces! But Clare was stronger, and Tommy knew that when Clare was roused, he would fight.

Finding his demonstration made no impression, Tommy took his knuckles out of his eyes and thrust them into his pocket-holes, turned his back on his friend, and began to whistle, with a lump of self-pity in his throat.

The boys turned their faces again toward the center of the town, and resumed their walk, still hungry, though not so hungry as they had been. The place looked wonderful to Clare, and his hopes of earning his bread grew yet more radiant. Up one street and down another the boys wandered, seeing plenty of food through windows, and in carts and baskets, but never any coming their way—except in the form of tempting odors that issued from almost every house, and grew in keenness and strength toward one o'clock.

As the evening came down upon them, the boys were

worn out, faint with want, shivering with cold, and miserable. They had to find shelter. As they walked about in their misery, white with cold and hunger, Clare's eyes kept turning to every archway, every breach in the wall or hedge, while Tommy would bolt from his side to peer into any opening. Once, in a lane on the outskirts of the town, Tommy darted into a narrow doorway in the face of a wall, but rushed back in horror. Within was a well where water lay still and dark. Then Clare first had a hint of the peculiar dread Tommy had of water, especially of water dark and unexpected.

It was an old town in which they were wandering, and many of the houses were withering and crumbling away— some from poverty, and some from utter disuse. The boys came out of the lane into the end of a wide silent street, where one house drew the roving, questing eyes of Clare and Tommy. Its windows were shuttered or broken; its roof was like the back of a very old horse; its chimney pots were jagged and stumped; from one of them, by its entangled string, the skeleton of a kite hung halfway down the front. But the red brick wall and the wrought iron gate, both seven feet high, stood in perfect aged strength. The house seemed to say to them, "There's nobody here—come in!" But the gate and the wall said, "Begone!"

CHAPTER EIGHT
The Forge

At the end of the wall was a rough boarded fence that led Clare and Tommy some fifty yards or so to a blacksmith's forge and hovel. Looking in, they saw the blacksmith working with his bellows.*

Clare, drawn by the glow of the fire, did not hesitate to go in. Tommy followed, keeping Clare well between him and the black-browed man.

"What do you want, gutter-toads?" he cried, glancing up and seeing them approach. "This ain't a hotel."

"But it's a splendid fire," Clare replied, looking into the man's face with a wan smile, "and we're so cold."

"What's that to me!" answered the man, who seemed ready to quarrel with anything. "I didn't make my fire to warm little devils like you!"

"No, sir," said Clare, "but we're both cold, and your fire is so beautiful. Would you let us stand beside it a minute or two, sir?"

"Why do you say *sir* to me, you preaching little humbug? Don't you see I'm a workingman?"

"Yes, and that's why. I think we ought to say *sir* and *ma'am* to every one that can do something we can't. Tommy and I can't make iron do what we please, and you can, sir! It would be a grand thing for us if we could! Then we could get something to eat, and somewhere to lie down."

"Could you? Look at me, now. I can do the work of two men, and can't get work for half a man!"

"That's a sad pity!" Clare said. "I wish I had work! Then I would bring you something to eat."

"Who said I hadn't enough to eat? I ain't come to that yet, young'un! What made you say that?"

"Because when I had work, I had plenty to eat, and now that I have nothing to do, I have nothing to eat. It's well I haven't work now, though," added Clare with a sigh, "for I'm too tired to do any. Please may I sit on this heap of ashes?"

"Sit where you like, so long 's you keep out o' my way. I ain't got nothing to give you but a bar of iron. I'll toast one for you if you would like a bite."

"No, thank you, sir," answered Clare, with a smile. "I'm afraid it wouldn't be digestible."

"You're a comical shaver, you are!" said the blacksmith. "You'll come to the gallows yet, if you're a good boy! Ain't that your brother?"

By this time Tommy had edged nearer to the fire, and now stood in the light of it.

"No," answered Clare.

"That ain't no pity—he'd ha' been no better than you. I've a brother I would choke any minute I got the chance."

The blacksmith's attention was caught by Tommy's gestures. He was making rapid signs to him, touching his forehead with one finger, nodding mysteriously, and pointing at Clare with the thumb of his other hand. The blacksmith understood that Tommy meant Clare was an idiot.

"Why do you let him follow you about, if he ain't your brother?" he said. "He ain't nice to look at."

"I want to make him nice," answered Clare, "and then he'll be nice to look at. He's a very little boy and ain't been well brought up. His granny ain't a good woman—at least not very, you know, Tommy!" he added apologetically.

"She's a dirty old sinner!" said Tommy stoutly.

The man laughed. "Ha, ha, my chicken! You know a thing or two!" he said, as he took his iron from the fire, and laid it again on the anvil.

But besides the brother he would so gladly strangle, there was an idiot one whom the blacksmith loved a little and teased so much that, when he died, his conscience was moved. He felt a little tenderness toward the idiot before him.

"Boys, if you ain't got nowhere to go to, I don't mind if you sleep here. There ain't no bed but the forge, nor no blankets but this leather apron: you may have them, for you can't do them no harm."

"Thank you, sir," said Clare.

The blacksmith covered the fire with coal and departed, locking the door of the smithy behind him.

Tommy turned to the bellows, and began to blow.

"Ain't you warm yet?" asked Clare.

"No, I ain't. I want a blaze."

"Leave the fire alone. The coal is the smith's—we should not waste it."

"He ain't no count!" said Tommy, as heartless as any grown man or woman set on pleasure.

"He has given us a place to be warm and sleep in! It would be a shame to do anything he didn't like. Have you no conscience, Tommy?"

"No," said Tommy, who did not know conscience from copper.

"If you have no conscience," answered Clare, "one must serve us both—as far as it will reach! Let go of that bellows, or I'll make you!"

Tommy let go, turned his back, and wandered to the other side of the shed. "Here's a door, and it ain't locked, only bolted! Let's go and see!"

"You may if you like," answered Clare, "but if you touch anything of the blacksmith's, I'll be down on you."

"All right!" said Tommy, and went out to see if there was anything to be picked up.

Clare lay down in the hot ashes on the stone hearth of the forge, far gone with hunger. He was soon fast asleep.

Tommy, out in the moonlight, found himself in a waste yard, scattered with bits of iron. He went shifting and nosing about everywhere, and presently he heard the sound of a hen. More stealthily yet he went creeping and feeling here and there and found her.

The hen sat still, and he concluded that under her might be eggs. Slipping his hand under her, Tommy found five eggs. In greedy haste he took them and sucked every one of them. But he made one mistake: he threw away the shells.

When he had sucked them, he was still just as hungry as before! The spirit of research began to move again in him. The moon was nearly full, and the smithy's yard was radiantly illuminated.

The enclosure was small—bounded on one side by the garden wall of the house they had just passed, and at the bottom by a broken fence, dividing it from a piece of waste land that probably belonged to the house. As he roamed about, Tommy spied a great heap of old iron piled against the wall. He scrambled to the top, and looked over. His gaze fell right into a big barrel, full of dark water. Tommy dared not cross at that point.

With much trembling he got on top of the wall, turned his back on the barrel, and ran along in search of a place where he could descend into the garden. He went right to the end, around the corner, and halfway along the bottom before he found one. There he came to a doorway that had been solidly walled up on the outside, while the door was left in position on the inside. Its frame was flush with the wall, so that its bolts and lock afforded Tommy foothold enough to descend, and confidence of being able to get up again.

He landed in a deserted garden. Tommy crept under the overgrown bushes until he reached a mossy walk that led him to the house. All the windows had outside shutters. Those on the ground floor were closed, except one that swung to and fro.

Tommy sought the window with the open shutter. Through the dirty glass, and its reflection of the moon, he could see nothing. He tried to open the window, but could not stir it. He went around the corner to one end of the house and saw another door. Suddenly, the moon shone up from the ground. In a hollow of the pavement a pool had gathered from the drip of the neglected gutters. Out of its hidden depth the staring moon looked at him.

It was the third time Tommy's nerves had been shaken that night, and he could stand no more. He turned and fled, fell, and rose and fled again. It was not imagination in Tommy—it was an undefined, inexplicable horror, that must have had a cause, but could have no reason. Only one material thing and two spiritual things had power with him: the one material thing was hunger, and the two spiritual things were a feeble love for Clare and a strong horror of water of any seeming depth.

Tommy rushed down the garden, found the prisoned door, gained the top of the wall, and sped along as if pursued. All at once the moon again looked up at him from below: he was within a yard or two of the big water barrel! Right up to it he must go, for there was the heap of iron by which alone he could get down. As he tightened every agonized nerve to stoop and kneel right over the water barrel, something dark and hideous and ghastly sprang right out of the water into the air with an appalling unearthly cry. Tommy tumbled from the wall among the iron, and lay there.

The stolen eggs were avenged. The unhappy hen had gone to the barrel to sip a little water. When Tommy startled her, she flew up with a screech, startled Tommy, and became her own unwitting avenger.

Clare woke from his sleep and looked about for Tommy. Surely it was time he had come back! Stiff and sore, he turned, crept down from the forge, and went out shivering. Picking his way among spikes and corners and edges of rusty iron, he walked about searching for Tommy, afraid to call for fear of attracting attention. He noted the scattered eggshells, but they told him nothing.

At last Clare came to the heap of metal, and there lay Tommy, caught in its skeleton protrusions. A shiver went through Clare when he saw the pallid face and the dark streak of blood across it. He took Tommy in his arms back to the smithy, and laid him on the hearth near the fire. At last, Tommy opened his eyes, scrambled to his feet, and stared wildly around him.

"Where is it?" he cried.

"Where's what?" rejoined Clare.

"The head that flew out of the water barrel," shuddered Tommy.

"Have you lost your senses, Tommy?" Clare asked. "I found you lying on a heap of old iron against the wall, with the moon shining on you."

"Yes, yes—the moon! She jumped out of the water barrel, and got ahold of me. I knew she would!"

"I didn't think you were such a fool, Tommy!" said Clare.

"Well, you hadn't the pluck to go yourself!" cried Tommy, putting his hand to his head, but more sorely hurt that an idiot should call him a fool. Tommy gradually recovered, and told Clare about the house he had discovered—but not what he had found.

"There's something yellow on your jacket!" Clare said. "You've been eating an egg! I remember that I saw eggshells lying in the yard, and the poor hen walking about looking for her eggs. You pig of a boy! I won't thrash you this time, because you've fetched your own thrashing. I believe it was the hen herself that frightened you," he added. "She served you right, you thief!"

"I didn't know there was any harm," said Tommy, pretending to sob.

"Why didn't you bring me my share, then?"

"'Cause I knew you'd ha' made me give 'em back to the hen!"

"Now, look here, Tommy! If you don't mind what I tell you, you and I part company. Do you hear me?"

"I can't do without food!" whimpered Tommy. "I didn't come wi' you to starve to death!"

"When I starve, you must starve too—and when I eat, you shall have the first mouthful. What did you come with me for?"

"'Cause you was the strongest," answered Tommy, "an' I reckoned you would get things from coves* we met."

"Well, I'm not going to get things from coves we meet, unless they give them to me. Have patience, Tommy, and I'll get you all you can eat. You must give me time, you know! I ain't got work yet! Come here. Lie down close to me, and we'll go to sleep."

Despite everything, they fell fast asleep. Soon they were roused by thunderous blows on the door. The air was a tumult of howling threats and curses.

Tommy understood at once. "It's the blacksmith! He's roaring drunk! Let's get out, Clare, before he murders us in our beds!"

"We ought to let him into his own house if we can," Clare replied, rising and going to the door. It was a good thing that he found no way of opening it, for every instant there came a kick against it that threatened to throw it from its lock and hinges. Tommy made for the rear, and Clare followed— prudent enough to close the back door behind them.

Outside Tommy led the way to the bottom of the yard, and over the fence into the waste ground, hoping to find some way to mount the wall. He could not face the water barrel, and so ran and doubled and spied, but could find no other foothold. Then Clare realized how Tommy had gotten over before, and that he must be afraid to go that way again. Clare turned and ran; Tommy followed, but with misgiving. Clare sprang up the heap, and Tommy climbed shuddering after him, urged on by the fear of the drunken blacksmith, and drawn on by the dread of being abandoned by Clare.

"Watch out for the water barrel, Clare!" he gasped. "An' gi' me a hand up."

The moment he had his foot on the wall, Tommy said, "Now let me go first! I know where to get down." He scudded along the wall, glad to have Clare between him and the barrel. Clare followed swiftly.

CHAPTER NINE
Treasure Trove

In a few moments they were safe in the thicket at the foot of the garden wall. Through the tangled thicket they found their way to the house.

Clare tried to get a peep through the window with the swinging shutter, but had no better success than Tommy. Then he started to go around the corner next to the blacksmith's yard.

"Look out!" cried Tommy in a loud whisper, when he saw where Clare was going. "There's a horrible hole there, full of water!"

"I'll keep a lookout," replied Clare. When he was about halfway along the end of the house, he heard a noise and stopped to listen. Someone was moving about somewhere. Then came a kind of scrambling sound, and a great watery splash. *Something has fallen into the water hole!* Clare said to himself, and ran on to see. A few steps brought him to what Tommy had taken for a great hole. It was only a pool of rainwater: the splash could not have come from that!

But the water barrel could not be far off. Clare forced his way through the shrubs, reached the wall, and went back along it until he came to the barrel. A ray of moonlight showed him that the side of it was wet, as if the water had just come over the edge. With the help of a small tree, he got on the wall and looked down. Spying into the barrel, he saw something white under the water, but floating near the surface. He lay down on the wall, plunged his arm into the barrel, and drew it out. It was a tiny baby in a flannel nightgown! It lay perfectly still in his arms, and Clare could not tell if the baby was dead or alive.

Clare stood in stony bewilderment. What was he to do? Certainly not go after the mother! The first thing was to get the baby down inside the wall! Clare started along the top of the wall, with the poor unconscious germ of humanity in his arms.

When he reached the door-ladder, he found descent difficult, but possible. It was more difficult to make his way through the tangled bushes without scratching the baby, which, after all, might be beyond hurt! Thus laden, he appeared before Tommy, who had heard the splash, had thought Clare had fallen into the deep hole, and still stood trembling where Clare had left him.

"Here, Tommy," Clare cried, "come and see what I found in the water barrel!"

"Oh, no, it's a kid!" he cried. "Put it in again," he said, with evil promptitude.

"But that would drown it, Tommy!" answered Clare, treating him like the child he was not. "We want it to live!"

"No, we don't!" returned Tommy. "What business has *it* to live when we can't get nothing to eat?"

Clare held fast to the baby with one arm, and with the fist of the other struck straight out at Tommy, hit him between the eyes, and knocked him flat. Tommy thus understood that the baby had rights—and if the baby could not enforce them, there was one in the world who could and would.

Tommy rose rubbing his forehead and crying quietly. Though he was not much hurt, from that moment he began to respect Clare.

The infant lay motionless, its little heart beating doubtfully.

"We *must* get into the house, Tommy!" Clare said.

"Yes, Clare," answered Tommy, very meekly, and went off to investigate the other end of the house. He was back in a moment, his face radiant with success. "Come, come!" he cried. "We can get in quite easy. I ha' *been* in!"

Tommy had found a long narrow cellar window with a

loose grating. He had lifted it, and pushed open the rusty-hinged window—but that he had been in was a lie. *He* knew better than to go in first!

Clare hurried after him.

"Gi' me the kid, an' you get in. You can reach up for it better, 'cause you're taller," said Tommy.

"Is it much of a drop?" asked Clare.

"Nothing much," answered Tommy.

Clare handed him the baby, telling him how to hold it, and threatening him if he hurt it. Then he laid himself on his front, shoved his legs and body through the window, let his feet as far down as he could, then dropped, fell on a heap of coals, and tumbled to the floor of the cellar.

"You should have told me about the coals!" he said, rising and calling up through the darkness.

"I forgot," answered Tommy.

"Give me the baby," said Clare.

When Tommy took the baby, he was tempted to throw it in the pool, and then make for the wall and the fields, leaving Clare to shift for himself. But he knew Clare would be sure to get out after him! So he stood with the hated creature in his unprotective arms.

When Clare called for it, Tommy pushed the baby through the window, grasped the extreme of its garment, and let it hang down headfirst into the darkness. Before Clare could reach it, the baby began to cry.

"Can't you let her down farther, Tommy?" Clare asked eagerly.

"No, I can't," answered Tommy. "Here—catch!"

Waiting for no sign from Clare, Tommy dropped the little one. It fell on Clare and knocked him over. But he clasped it to him as he fell, and they hurtled to the bottom of the coals without much damage.

"I have her!" he cried as he got up. "Now you come yourself, Tommy."

Clare had known no baby but his lost sister, and thought of all babies as girls.

"You'll catch me, won't you, Clare?" Tommy asked.

"No, I can't put down the baby to catch you!" replied Clare, and turned to seek an exit from the cellar.

Tommy came tumbling on the top of the coals. "Where are you, Clare?" he called.

Clare answered him from the top of the stone stair that led to the cellar, and Tommy was soon at his heels. Feeling their way along a dark passage, they arrived at the kitchen. The loose outside shutter belonged to it, and a little of the moonlight came in. The place looked dreary and cold with its damp brick floor and its rusty range. If only they had some way to light a fire with the coals.

"I don't see as we're much better off!" said Tommy. "I'm cold as can be!"

"Then what must the baby be like!" said Clare, whose heart was full of anxiety for his charge.

"We needn't stay here, though," he said. "There must be better places in the house!" They left the kitchen, and went up the stairs and into the first room they came to. It was a bedroom—larger and grander than any at the parsonage.

Clare walked over to examine the bed. The bedspread was very dusty—and oh, such moth-eaten blankets! But there were sheets under them—quite clean, though dingy with age. The moths—that is, their legs and wings and dried up bodies—flew out in clouds when Clare moved the blankets. Nonetheless, Clare and Tommy discovered Paradise!

With deft hands Clare took off the infant's one garment, gently rubbed her little body till it was quite dry (if not very clean), laid her tenderly in the heart of the blankets, and covered her up, leaving a little opening for her to breathe through. He threw off his clothes, and got into the mothy blankets beside her. He took the baby in his arms and held her close to his body.

"Now, Tommy," he said, "you may get in on the other side of me."

Tommy did not need a second invitation, and in a moment they were all fast asleep.

CHAPTER TEN
Breakfast

Though as comfortable as one could be who so rarely lacked food, Clare slept lightly. He woke very early with anxious thoughts. Babies always had their food given to them; therefore babies who didn't have food had a right to ask for it. Yet babies couldn't ask for it, therefore those who took care of them, and didn't have food to give them had a right to do the asking for them. Clare could not beg for himself as long as he was able to ask for work; but for the baby it was his duty to beg, because she would not live till he found work. If he got work that very day, he would have to work the whole day before he got paid—and the baby would be dead by that time!

Clare crept out, so as to not wake the sleepers, and put on his clothes. He did not at all like leaving the baby with Tommy, but what was he to do? She might as well die of Tommy as of hunger!

He searched the house and found two empty medicine bottles. He chose the smaller, then woke Tommy, and said, "I am going out to get baby's breakfast."

"Ain't you going to give *me* any? Is the kid to have *everything?*"

"Tommy!" Clare said, with a steady look in his eyes that frightened him, "your turn will come next. You won't die of hunger for a day or two yet. I'll see to you as soon as I can. Only remember, the baby comes first! I am going to leave her with you. But if, when I come home, I find anything has happened to her, *I'll put you in the water barrel*—I WILL! And I'll do it when the moon is in it!"

Tommy made a hideous face and began to yell. Clare seized him by the throat.

"Make that noise again, you rascal, and I'll choke you! If you're good to the baby while I'm away, I won't eat a mouthful till you've had some; if you're not good to her, you know what will happen!" Clare left Tommy with his treasure, and set out on his quest.

He got out through the kitchen. He dared not go along the wall in the daylight, or get down in the blacksmith's yard, so he dropped straight to the ground.

The country was level, and he saw a farm nearby. He knew cows were milked early, so he set out to run straight across the fields. But he soon found he could not run, and had to drop into a walk.

When Clare got into the yard, he saw a girl carrying a foaming pail of milk across to the dairy. He followed her, and looking into the dairy, saw an elderly woman.

"Please, ma'am, could you give me as much fresh milk as would fill this bottle?" he asked, showing it.

"Well, I think we might. But what on earth made you bring such a small bottle?"

"It's for a very little baby. I think it will hold enough to keep her alive till I get work."

The woman looked, and her heart was drawn to the boy.

"How old's the baby?" she asked.

"I don't know, ma'am; she only came to us last night."

"Who brought her?"

"I don't know, ma'am. I took her out of the water barrel."

"Who put her there?"

"I don't know, ma'am."

"Whose baby is she, then?"

"Mine, I think, ma'am."

"God bless the boy!" said the woman impatiently, and stared at him speechless.

Her daughter filled the bottle with new milk, and handed it to Clare. "Oh, thank you, ma'am!" he said. "But, please, would you tell me how much water I must put in the milk to make it good for the baby? I know it wants water, but I don't know how much!"

"Oh, about half and half," the woman answered. "Ain't she got no mother?"

"I think she must have a mother, but I don't know where she is," answered Clare.

"Wouldn't you like some milk yourself?" she said.

"Oh, yes, ma'am!" answered Clare, with a deep sigh.

She filled a big cup for him from the warm milk in the pail. Clare lifted it to his lips, then let his hand sink—trembling so that he spilled a little. His promise to Tommy had sprung upon him like a fiery serpent. "Please, ma'am, there's Tommy!" he faltered.

"Tommy? I thought you said the baby was a girl."

"Yes, the *baby's* a girl—but there's *Tommy* as well! He's another of us."

"Your brother, of course!"

"No, ma'am—I'm afraid he's a tramp. He has no one to care for him, you see, and I promised to share with him."

Just then the farmer's gruff, loud voice came from the yard. He was a bitter-tempered man, and his dislike of tramps was almost hatred.

"There's the master!" cried the mother. "Drink, and hurry out of here."

"If it's stealing—" said Clare.

"Stealing? It's not stealing. The dairy's mine!"

"Well, ma'am, if the milk's mine because you gave it to me, it's not begging to ask you to give me a piece of bread to go with it! I could take a share of that to Tommy."

"Run, Chris!" cried the mother to the girl. "Take this boy with you—outside the yard. Give him some bread, and let him go. For God's sake, don't let your father see him!"

There was a little passage and another door, by which they left as the farmer entered. The girl ran with him to the back of the house, handed Clare a whole loaf of homemade bread, and told him to run for his life. She disappeared before he could thank him.

With the farmer behind, and the hungry ones before him, Clare *did* run—with the bottle in his pocket and the loaf in his hands. But Clare's jubilation ended when he reached the abandoned house. It was one thing to drop from the wall, and quite another to climb to the top of it without the help of the door! He heard the clink of the blacksmith's hammer on his anvil, and to go by his yard in daylight would be to risk too much! Clare stood at the foot of the brick wall and stared up with helpless eyes. Next he prowled all along the bottom of the garden, and then up the narrow lane between it and the garden of the next house.

A dozen yards or so from the end of the lane, Clare spied an opening in the wall—the same from which, the night before, Tommy had returned with such a frightened face. Clare went through it, and found a narrow passage running to the left for a short distance between two walls. At the end, half on one side, half on the other of the second wall, lay the well that had terrified Tommy. The wall crossed it with a low arch, and on the further side of the well was a third wall, with a space of about two feet and a half between it and the side of the round well. Through that wall there might be a door. If not, there might be some way of getting over it.

Clare tied the loaf in his handkerchief, and knotted the ends around his neck. He got on his knees on the parapet. How deep and dark the water looked! For a moment, he felt a fear of something like Tommy's. How should he cross the awful gulf? It was not like a free jump, for he was hemmed in before and behind, and overhead also. He made a cat leap through beneath the arch, reaching out with his hands and catching the parapet beyond. He caught just enough of it so that his body did not follow his legs into the cold water. Straining and heaving, he made a great reach across the parapet with one hand, laid hold of its outer edge, and pulled himself out of the water and the well.

He was in a narrow space, closed in with walls much higher than his head. Presently, he saw that by leaning his back against one wall, pushing his feet against the opposite wall, and making of the third wall a rack for his shoulder, he could worm himself slowly up. He fell to, and with an agony of exertion, wriggled himself at last to the top, and dropped into the garden—exhausted, and with his clothes badly torn.

Clare shot up the stairs and found both Tommy and the baby fast asleep. He woke Tommy, and showed him the loaf. Tommy sprang from his lair and snatched it.

"No, Tommy," Clare said, drawing back, "you must wait till I've fed the baby."

There was but one way to feed her—as the pigeons do. Clare laid the baby down again and fetched water from the pool. He mixed the milk with what seemed the right amount of water, took the baby up, laid a folded blanket on his knees, and laid her in her blanket upon it. Then he took a small mouthful of the milk and water, and held it until it grew warm. Then he put his mouth to the baby's; she managed to swallow the mouthful successfully. It was followed by a second, a third, and more, until the child seemed satisfied. He put her in the bed again, and covered her up. All the time, Tommy had been watching the loaf with the eyes of a wild beast.

"Now, Tommy," said Clare, "how much of this loaf do you think you ought to have?"

"Half, of course!" answered Tommy boldly.

"Are you as big as I am?"

Tommy held his peace.

"You ain't half as big!" said Clare.

"I'm a bloomin' lot hungrier!" growled Tommy.

"You had eggs last night, and I had none!"

"That wurn't my fault!"

"What did you do to get this bread?"

"I stayed at home with the baby."

"That's true," answered Clare. "But," he went on, "suppose a horse and pony had to divide their food between them, would the pony have a right to half? Wouldn't the horse, being bigger, need more to keep him alive than the pony?"

"Don't know," said Tommy.

"But you shall have the half," continued Clare, "only I hope, after this, when you get anything given to you, you'll divide it with me. I try to be fair, and I want *you* to be fair."

Clare carefully divided the loaf, and after due deliberation, handed Tommy the bigger half. Without a word of acknowledgment, Tommy fell upon it like a terrier.

"Now, Tommy," Clare said, having eaten his share of the loaf, "I'm going out to look for work, and you must take care of the baby. You're not to feed her—you would only choke her, and waste the rest of the milk."

"I want to go out too," said Tommy.

"To see what you can pick up, I suppose?"

"That's my business."

"I fancy it mine while you are with me. If you don't take care of the baby and be good to her, I'll put you in the water barrel I took her out of."

"I *want* to go with you!" whimpered Tommy.

"You can't. You're to look after the baby. I won't be away longer than I can help." With repeated injunctions to him not to leave the room, Clare went.

But before he left the yard, Clare decided to arrange for his returning. Looking around, he caught sight of an old garden-roller, and was making for it, when Tommy, never doubting that Clare was gone, came whistling around the corner of the house with his hands in his pocket-holes, and an impudent air of independence.

Clare saw him before he saw Clare, and rushed at him with a roar. "You thought I was gone!" he cried. "I *told* you not to leave the room! Come along to the water barrel!"

Tommy shivered when he heard him, and gave a shriek when he saw him coming. As Clare came running, Tommy took one step toward him and dropped to the ground on his feet. Clare shot away over his head, struck his own against a tree, and lay for a minute stunned. Tommy rushed into the house, and bolted the kitchen door.

When Clare came to himself, he found he had a cut on his

head. It would never do to go asking for work with a bloody face! The little pool served as a basin and mirror, and while he washed he thought. He had no plan to punish Tommy for the trick—he had only done the natural thing. It would serve a good end too. Tommy would imagine him lurking about for revenge and would not venture his nose out. Clare discovered afterward that Tommy had fastened the cellar door, so that if he had entered that way, he would have been caught in a trap, unable to go or return.

He wrestled the iron roller to the foot of the wall, where he had come over earlier, and where now he perceived there had once been a door. He set it on end, filled it with earth, and heaped a mound of earth about it to steady it, then placed a few broken tiles and shards of chimney pots upon it. From this rickety perch, Clare found he could reach the top easily.

Next he threw over the wall earth and stones and whatever rubbish came to his hand. The narrow walls kept the heap confined, and he made good speed. At length he descended by it, now sure of being able to get up again.

He had been gone an hour before Tommy dared again to leave the room where the baby was. He had planned what to do if Clare came into the room: he would threaten, if he came a step nearer, to kill the baby! But if Clare was trapped in the coal cellar, Tommy would make his own conditions!

Finally, Tommy opened the bedroom door slowly and carefully. He saw no one, and crept out. By slow degrees, he got down the stairs and went out into the garden. There he was satisfied that Clare had departed. For a time, Tommy was his own master. What was he to do? Go after something to eat, of course! And what harm would come to the brat? She was not able to roll herself off the bed, and she could do nothing but go to sleep again.

He ran down to the garden, scrambled up the door, got on the top of the wall, and dropped into the wasteland behind it—never thinking that his only way back was past the water barrel.

CHAPTER ELEVEN

The Baker and the Draper

Clare went over the wall and the well without a notion of what he was going to do, except look for work.

Within a hundred yards, Clare came to a baker's shop. He went in, not knowing it was the shop from whose cart Tommy had pilfered. A thin-faced, bilious-looking elderly man stood behind the counter.

"Well, boy, what do you want?" he asked in a low voice.

"Please, sir," answered Clare, "I want work to do, and I thought perhaps you could help me."

"What can you do?"

"Not much, but I can try to do anything."

"Have you ever learned to do anything?"

"I've been working on a farm, because my parents died."

"Why did you leave the farm?"

"Because they didn't want me. The farmer's wife didn't like me."

"I dare say she had her reasons!"

"I don't know, sir. She didn't seem to like anything I did."

"So the farmer sent you away?"

"No, sir, but he boxed my ears for something."

"I dare say you deserved it!"

"Perhaps I did. I don't know, but I didn't run away for that, sir. I ran away because he was tired of me. I couldn't stay to make him uncomfortable! He had been very kind to me, and I fancy it was the mistress who made him change. I'm very sorry not to have him or the creatures anymore."

"What creatures?"

"The bull, the horses, the cows, and the pigs—all the

creatures about the farm. They were my friends, and I loved them." He gave a great sigh.

"You *can't* love a bull, or a horse, or a pig!" asserted the baker.

"But I *do*," rejoined Clare. "I love my father and my mother much more than when they were alive!"

"What has that got to do with it?" returned the baker.

"That I know I love my father and mother, and I know I love that fierce old bull that would always do what I told him, and that dear old horse that was almost past work, and was always there to do his best—I'm afraid they've killed him by now!" Clare added, with another sigh.

"But beasts ain't got souls, and you can't love them. And if you could, that's no reason why you should see them again."

"I suppose you don't like animals, sir! Are you afraid of their going to the same place as you when they die?"

"I wouldn't have a boy about me that held such an unscriptural notion! The Bible says that the spirit of a man goeth upward, and the spirit of a beast goeth downward!"

"I didn't know there was anything about it in the Bible! Then when I die I shall only have to go downward somewhere, and look for them till I find them!"

The baker was silenced for a moment, and then cried, "It's flat atheism! Get out of my shop!"

Clare turned and went out.

But the baker was not usually an unreasonable or unjust man. He vaulted over the counter, opened the door, and shouted after Clare.

The boy went meekly back.

"I've just remembered hearing," the baker said, "that one of Mr. Maidstone's errand boys is laid up with scarlet fever. I'll take you to him, if you like. I don't promise you, but perhaps he'll have you, though I can't say you look respectable!"

"I ain't had much chance since I left home, sir. I had a bit of soap, but—" He thought that he had better say nothing about his family. Clare had hidden his soap, but when he went to find it, it was gone.

"You see, sir," he resumed, "I had other things to think of. When your tummy's empty, you don't think about the rest of you—do you, sir?"

The baker could not remember having ever been more than decently, healthily hungry in his life. "I don't know, my boy," he answered. "Would you like a piece of bread?"

"I'm not much in want of it at this moment," replied Clare, "but I should be greatly obliged if you would let me call for it by and by."

The baker called to someone inside to mind the shop, removed his apron and put on a coat, shut the door, and went down the street with Clare to the shop of a draper* and haberdasher.* He asked to see Mr. Maidstone, who came out into the public floor.

"I heard you were in need of a boy, sir," said the baker, who carried himself as in the presence of a superior. And certainly fine clothes and a gold chain and ring did what they could to make the draper superior to the baker.

"Hm!" said Mr. Maidstone, looking with contempt at Clare. "He don't look promising."

"He don't. But I think he means performing," said the baker with a wan smile.

"If he 'appened to wash his face, I could tell better."

"He says he's been too hungry to wash his face," answered the baker.

"Will you answer for him, Mr. Ball?"

"I can't, Mr. Maidstone—not one way or another. I simply was taken with him. I know nothing about him."

Here one of the shopmen came up to the master and said, "I heard Mr. Ball's own man yesterday accuse this very boy of taking a loaf from his cart."

"Oh! *This* is the boy, is it?" said the baker. "All the same, I don't believe he took the loaf."

"Indeed I didn't, sir!" said Clare. "Another boy took it who didn't know better, and I took it from him, and was putting it back on the cart when the man turned round and saw me, and wouldn't listen to a word I said. But a workingman believed me, and bought the loaf for us."

"A likely story!" said the draper.

"I've heard that much," said the baker, "and I believe it. At least I have no reason to believe my man against him, Mr. Maidstone. That same night I discovered he had been cheating me to a merry tune. I discharged him this morning."

"Well, you certainly don't look like a respectable boy," said the draper, who naturally, being all surface himself, could read no deeper than clothes. "But I need someone to carry out parcels, and I'll try you. If you steal anything, you'll be caught within the hour! You shall have sixpence a day," Mr. Maidstone continued, "and not a penny more till I'm sure you're honest."

"Thank you, sir!" said Clare. "Please may I run home first? I won't be long. I ain't got any other clothes, but—"

"Hold your tongue. Don't let me hear it wagging in my establishment. Go and wash your face and hands."

Clare turned to the baker, "Please, sir," he said softly, "may I go back with you and get the piece of bread?"

"What? Begging already?" cried Mr. Maidstone.

"No, no, sir," interposed the baker. "I promised him a piece of bread. He did not ask for it."

The baker was pleased at his success, and regarded Clare with the favor that springs in the heart of him who has done a good turn to another through a third.

"I am so much obliged to you, sir!" said Clare as they went away together. "I cannot tell you how much!"

"Thank me by minding Mr. Maidstone's interests," returned the baker. "If you don't do well by him, the blame will come upon me."

"I will be very careful, sir," answered Clare, who was too full of honesty to think of being honest. He thought only of minding orders.

At his shop, the baker gave Clare a small loaf, and he hurried home with it.

CHAPTER TWELVE
The Family Grows

The door to the kitchen was open, and Clare found the baby alone, wailing piteously. He threw down the clothes to take her, and a great rat sprang from the bed. On one of the baby's tiny feet the long thin toes were bleeding and raw. A scampering and scuffling and squealing arose behind him in the room, and Clare's heart quivered.

Suddenly, the noise ceased with a sharp scream. Clare turned with the baby in his arms. At his feet, gazing up at him, stood a little castaway dog, the rat hanging limp from his jaws! His eyes flamed, and his tail wagged with wild homage and the delight of presenting the rat to one he would make his master.

"You darling!" cried Clare. The dog dropped the dead rat at his feet, but would not touch the rat until Clare told him to take it. Then he retired with it to a corner, and made a rapid meal of it.

Clare gave the baby what milk and water was left. Then he washed her poor torn foot, wrapped it in a pillowcase, and laid her in the bed. Next he cut a good big crust from the loaf and gave it to the dog, and the rest he put in a drawer. Then he washed his face and hands as well as he could without soap. After that, he took the dog, talked to him a little, and laid him on the bed beside the baby. Clare told the dog that he was to care for the baby, that he must watch and tend and, if needed, fight for the little one. Then he left, for it was plain to Clare that the dog understood his duty thoroughly.

Once clear of the well and the wall, Clare set off running.

When he returned to the shop, Mr. Maidstone handed him a large package and said, "Take this parcel to Mrs. Trueman's. You'll see the address on it. And look sharp."

The parcel was of considerable size. Clare stooped a little as he balanced its weight on his shoulder. Holding it in place with one hand, he started for the door, which the master himself held open for him.

"Please, sir, which way do I turn?" he asked.

"To the left," answered Mr. Maidstone. "Ask your way as you go."

Clare had heard only the lady's name. Her address was on the parcel, but if he dropped it to look, he could not get it up again by himself. Therefore, he asked a passing boy to read the address on his back and direct him. The boy read it aloud, but gave him false instructions. Clare walked and walked until the weight became almost unendurable, and at last concluded that the boy had deceived him. He asked again, but this time of a lady. She took pains to tell him which way to go. Following her directions, he found the house. But it was hours after the burden was gone from his shoulder before he was rid of the phantom of its weight.

Mr. Maidstone scolded Clare for having been so long, and would not permit him to explain his delay. The rest of the day's work was lighter, and he gained something more than a general idea of how the streets lay. He was weary when, with the sixpence his master gave him, he set out at last for Mr. Ball's and the milk shop. Of the former he bought a stale five-penny loaf, and the other penny he laid out on milk. The milk woman graciously granted him the two matches he begged for.

At the house, Clare found the infant and the dog lying as he had left them. He got some sticks together from the garden, and with one of the precious matches, lit a small fire of coals. And the day held yet another gladness: in looking for a kettle, he found his soap. He filled the rusty kettle with water, and while it was growing hot on the fire, he ran out every other minute to see how much smoke was coming from the chimney, lest it should betray them.

Now at last Clare was equipped to wash the baby. With a basin of warm water and his precious piece of soap he set about it, and taking much pains washed the baby perfectly clean. His chief anxiety was not to hurt the poor rat-eaten little toes. When the happy task was over, he wrapped her in another blanket, and laid her down again. Soothed and comforted as perhaps never before, she went to sleep.

He took a piece of bread for the dog, which the small hero, whose four legs carried such a long barrel of starvation, ate with undisguised pleasure and thankfulness. Clare followed his dry-bread supper with a cup of water from the well.

Darkness had fallen. Weary to the very bones, Clare threw himself on the bed beside the baby. The dog jumped up and laid himself at his feet. There the three of them fell fast asleep.

Tommy had not had a very happy day: he had been caught in evildoing, had done more evil, and had all the day been in dread of punishment. He had deserted the baby in the hope of finding something to eat, but had not had a mouthful of anything but a spongy turnip and a dried-up beet root. He had been set upon by boys bigger than himself and nearly as bad. They bullied Tommy in a way that would have been to his heart's content, had he been the bully instead of the bullied. They made him wish he had stayed with the baby—and therewith came the thought that it was time to go home if he would get back before Clare. Off went Tommy for home. But as he ran he remembered that the way into the house was by the very lip of the water barrel.

Clare woke up suddenly. He could hear the whimpering of a child. However, the baby was fast asleep, and Clare thought instantly of Tommy—shut out in the night, and not daring to go near the water barrel! Clare jumped out of bed, put on his shoes, and was soon over the wall and walking along the lane outside of it.

The night was dark, yet Clare saw Tommy crouching against the wall. "Tommy!" he said softly.

Tommy did not reply. The fear of the water barrel was upon him.

"Tommy, I see you, you bad boy!" whispered Clare. "After all I said, you ran away and left the baby to the rats! One has been biting her horribly. You can stay away as long as you like now—I've got a better nurse. Good night!"

Tommy gave a great howl.

"Hold your tongue, you rascal!" whispered Clare. "You'll let the police know where we are!"

"Do let me in, Clare! I'm so 'ungry and so cold!"

"Then I shall have to put you in the water barrel! I said I would."

"If you don't promise not to, I'll go straight to the police. They'll take the brat from you, and put her in the workhouse!"*

Clare thought for a moment. "Tommy, I forgive you for leaving the baby," he said solemnly, "and will be friends with you again. But I have said it, and into the water barrel you must go! I can't trust your word now, but I think I shall be able to trust it after that."

Tommy lifted up his voice in a most unearthly screech, but Clare grasped him by the throat so that he could not utter a sound. "Tommy," he said, "I'm going to let you breath again, but the moment you make a noise, I'll choke you."

With that, he relaxed his hold. But Tommy had paid no heed to what he had said, and began a second screech. Immediately he was choked, and after two or three attempts, finally desisted. Clare threw him over his shoulder, and took him around the wall and over the fence into the blacksmith's yard. The smithy was quite dark.

"Please, I didn't mean to do it!" sobbed Tommy. "I didn't mean to leave the baby!"

Clare stopped. "How did you do it, then?"

"I mean I didn't mean to stay away so long. I didn't know how to get back."

"I told you not to leave her! And you could have come

back easily, you little coward!"

Tommy shuddered, and said no more. They came to the heap, and there was only that and the wall between him and the water barrel. Up and up he felt himself slowly carried, then Clare, having reached the top, seated himself on the wall with his legs alongside the water barrel. Then he drew Tommy from his shoulder, in spite of his clinging, and laid him across his knees. Tommy remained silent.

"Your hour is come, Tommy!" said Clare. "If you scream I will drop you in, and hold you by one leg. If you don't scream, I will hold you by both legs. If you scream when I take you out, in you go again!"

The wretched boy was nearly mad with terror. But now, much as he feared the water, he feared Clare more. Clare took him by the heels, let him hang for a moment over the black water, and then forced him down to the neck in the water. Lifted out again, he spluttered and gurgled and tried to scream.

"Now, Tommy," said Clare, "don't scream, or I'll put you in again."

Tommy screamed, and was put in the water again; the next time he was taken out, he did not scream. Clare laid him down on the wall, and he lay still, pretending to be drowned. Clare got up, set him on his feet in front of him, and holding him by his collar, trotted him round the top of the wall, and dropped him into the garden. Tommy was quiet enough now—more than subdued, and incapable even of meditating revenge. He was now thoroughly afraid of Clare. When they entered the nursery, the dog took Tommy for a worse sort of rat and leaped at him as if he would swallow him alive. Tommy cried out in terror.

"Quiet, Abdiel!" said Clare.

The dog turned, jumped up on the bed, and lay down close to the baby. Clare had already given him the name of Abdiel, taken from *Paradise Lost.*

"Please, I couldn't help yelling!" said Tommy meekly. "I didn't know you'd gotten *him!*"

"I know you couldn't help it!" answered Clare. "What have you had to eat today?"

"Nothing but a beastly turnip and a wormy beet," said Tommy. "I'm awful hungry."

"You'd have had something better if you'd stuck by the baby, and not left her to the rats!"

"There ain't no rats," growled Tommy.

"Will you believe your own eyes?" returned Clare, and showed him the skin of the rat Abdiel had slain. "I've a great mind to make you eat it!" he added, dangling it before him by the tail.

"Shouldn't mind," said Tommy. "I've eaten a rat afore now, an' I'm that hungry! Rats ain't so bad to eat. I don't know about their skins."

"Here's a piece of bread for you. But you won't sleep with honest people like the baby and Abdiel. You will sleep on the hearth rug. Here's a blanket and pillow for you."

Clare covered Tommy up and he was soon asleep.

Clare's next day went much as the preceding. When his dinner hour came, he ran home and was glad to find Tommy and the dog mildly agreeable to each other. He had time only to give the baby some milk, and Tommy and Abdiel a bit of bread each.

Clare's look when he returned to the shop made one of the girls ask him what he had had for dinner. He said he had had none.

"Why?"

"Because there wasn't any."

"Didn't your mother keep some for you?"

"No, she couldn't."

"Then what will you do?"

"Go without," answered Clare with a smile.

"But you've got a mother?" said the girl, rendered doubtful by his smile.

"Oh, yes! I've got two mothers. But their arms ain't long enough," replied Clare.

The girl wondered if Clare was an idiot, or what they

called a poet. Anyhow, she had once been hungry for two weeks herself, and now had a bun in her pocket, and she offered him that.

"But what will you do yourself? Have you another?" asked Clare, unready to take it.

"No," she answered. "Why shouldn't I go without as well as you?"

"Because it won't make things any better. There will be just as much hunger. It's only shifting it from me to you, and that will leave it all the same!"

"No, not the same," she returned. "I've had a good dinner—as much as I could eat, and you've had none!"

Clare was persuaded, and ate the bun with much satisfaction and gratitude.

When he had his wages in the evening, he spent them as before—a penny for the baby, and fivepence at Mr. Ball's for Tommy, Abdiel, and himself. Observing that he came daily, and spent all but one penny of his wages on bread—seeing also that the boy's cheeks, though plainly he was in good health, were very thin—Mr. Ball wondered a little. A boy ought to look better than that on fivepence of bread a day!

They were a curious family—Clare, Tommy, the baby, and Abdiel. The only thing sad about it was that Clare, who was the head and the heart of it, and provided for all, should be upheld by no human sympathy, no human gratitude. But he had both sympathy and gratitude from Abdiel. The dog never failed to understand what Clare wished and expected him to understand. In Clare's absence he took on himself the protection of the establishment, and was Tommy's superior.

One day a bale of goods was unpacked in Clare's presence, and he begged the head shopman for a piece of the canvas wrapping. Mrs. Porson had taught Clare to sew, and with the help of a needle and thread the friendly shop girl gave him, he made a pair of trousers for Tommy, and a primitive shirt for himself, which he wore beneath the tatters of his jacket and trousers.

CHAPTER THIRTEEN
Gains and Losses

Things went on for nearly a month, everyone thriving but Clare.

One day a lady, attracted by a low-priced muff in the shop window, entered and asked to see it.

"I hope you will excuse me, madam," returned the shopman. "The muff is in a position hard to reach. Besides, we must ask leave to take anything down after the window is dressed for the day, and the master is out. But I will bring you another fur exactly like that one."

So saying he went and returned with a load of muffs and other furs, which he threw on the counter. But the lady persisted in demanding a sight of the muff in the window. The muff was hooked down and brought to her—not graciously. She glanced at it, turned it over, looked inside, and said, "I will take it. Please bring a bandbox* for it."

"I will, madam," said the man, and would have taken the muff. But she held it fast, sought her purse, and laid the price on the counter. The shopman saw that she knew what both of them were about, took up the money, went and fetched a bandbox, put the muff in it before her eyes, and tied it up. The lady held out her hand for it.

"Shall I send it to you, madam?" he asked.

"No," she answered. "I am on my way to the station."

"Here," cried the shopman to Clare, "take this bandbox, and go with that lady to the station."

The lady was about to insist on carrying the bandbox herself. But when Clare smiled up in her face, she knew she could trust him. The man stood watching for the moment when she should turn her back, because he was hoping to substitute another bandbox for the one Clare carried. But Clare walked straight out of the shop after the lady.

They had gone about halfway to the station, when from a side street came another boy from Mr. Maidstone's. He carried a box exactly like the one Clare had in his hand, and came softly up behind him.

"Look spry!" he said in a whisper. "She don't twig! It's all right! Maidstone sent me."

Clare looked around. The boy held out his bandbox for Clare to take, and his empty hand to take Clare's instead. But Clare had by this time begun to learn a little caution. Besides, the lady's interests were in his care, and he could not trick her behind her back! He held fast to the box. The boy gave him a great punch, but Clare clung even harder to the box. The lady heard something, and turned her head. The other boy was already walking away, but she saw that Clare's face was flushed.

"What is the matter?" she asked.

"I don't know, ma'am. He wanted me to give him my bandbox for his, and said Mr. Maidstone had sent him. But I couldn't, you know, except he asked you first. You did pay for it, didn't you?"

"Of course I did, or he wouldn't have let me take it away! But if you don't know what it means, I do. You haven't been in that shop long, have you?"

"Not over a month, ma'am."

"I thought so!" She said no more, and Clare followed in wondering silence. When they reached the station she searched her purse for a shilling.* She was unable to find one, and gave him a half crown* instead.

"You had better not mention that I gave you anything," she said.

"I will not, ma'am, except they ask me," he answered. "But is all this for me?"

"To be sure," she answered. "I am much obliged to you for—for carrying my parcel. Be an honest boy whatever comes, and you will not be sorry."

"I will try, ma'am," said Clare.

When his messenger came back to the store with the tale of how he had been foiled, Mr. Maidstone said nothing, but his lips grew white. He closed them fast, and went and stood near the door. When Clare opened it, he was met by a blow that dazed him, and a fierce kick that sent him on his back to the curb. Clare returned to the door and opened it a little. His master's face, with a hateful sneer upon it, shot into the crack, and spit in his face. Then the door shut sharply on his fingers. At last Clare understood: he had lost his job and his day's wages!

But he still had the half crown the lady had given him. He bought a bigger loaf than usual and went home. But Clare had made another enemy—the boy who had attempted to switch the bandboxes. He followed Clare all the way home, waiting to pounce upon him. He saw Clare turn in at the opening that led to the well, and thought he had him. But when he followed him in, Clare was not to be seen! He did not care to cross the well, not knowing what might meet him on the other side, but here was news to carry back! He did so, and Mr. Maidstone seized the opportunity to invalidate whatever Clare might reveal against him.

Clare and the baby and Tommy and Abdiel had eaten their supper and were all asleep. It was just past ten o'clock when Abdiel jumped up, cocked his ears, leaped off the bed to the door, and began barking furiously. He suddenly received a kick that knocked all the bark out of him and threw him to the other side of the room. A huge policeman walked quietly in, sending the glare of his lantern all about the room, and discovering, one after the other, every member of the family. So tired was Clare, however, that he did not wake until he was grabbed by a rough hand.

The policeman roused Tommy, who was pretending to be asleep, with a gentle kick. "Up ye get!" he said, and Tommy got up, rubbing his eyes.

"Come along!" said the policeman.

"Where to?" asked Clare.

"You'll see when you get there."

"But I can't leave the baby!"

"The baby must come along too," answered the policeman.

"But she has no clothes to go in!" objected Clare. "And the blanket I keep her in ain't mine—I can't take it with me."

"You don't mind takin' a 'ole 'ouse an' garden, but you wouldn' think o' taking' a blanket! Honest boy *you* are!"

"We've done the house no harm," said Clare, "and I will *not* take the blanket. It would be stealing!"

"Then *I* will take it, and be accountable for it," rejoined the man.

Clare went to the baby. He wrapped her closer in her blanket, and took her in his arms. He could not help her crying, but she was not strong enough to scream.

"Get along," said the policeman.

Clare led the way with his bundle, though the corners of the blanket kept working from his hold and trailing on the ground. Behind him came Tommy and the policeman trailed by the thin, long-bodied, short-legged Abdiel.

They came at last to the *lock-up** where the inspector charged them with housebreaking. Then they were taken away to the lock-up—all but the faithful Abdiel, who received another kick. The door was shut upon them, and they had to rest in that grave till the morning.

The dawn came, and at long last came the big policeman. To Clare's loving eyes, how friendly he looked!

"Come," he said, and took them through a long passage to a room in the town hall, where a formal-looking old gentleman sat behind a table.

"Good morning, sir," said Clare, to the astonishment of the magistrate, who thought the boy was showing disrespect.

"Hold your impudent tongue!" said a second policeman, and gave Clare a cuff on his head.

"Hold, John," interposed the magistrate. "It is *my* part to punish, not yours."

"Thank you, sir," said Clare.

"I will thank *you,* sir," returned the magistrate, "not to speak till I question you. What is the charge against the prisoners?"

"Housebreaking, sir," answered the big policeman.

"Housebreaking! Boys with a baby? Housebreakers don't generally go about with babies in their arms! Explain."

The policeman said he had received information that unlawful possession had been taken of a building which had been in chancery* for many years. He had gone to see, and had found the accused in the best bedrooms—fast asleep, surrounded by indications that they had made themselves a home there for some time.

The magistrate turned his eyes on Clare. "Is this true?"

"Yes, sir," answered Clare.

"What right did you have to be there?"

"None, sir. But we had nowhere else to go, and nobody seemed to want the place. We didn't hurt anything. We swept away a multitude of dead moths, and killed a lot of live ones, and the dog killed a great rat."

"What is your name?"

"Clare—Porson," answered Clare.

"Is that boy your brother?"

"No, sir. He's no relation of mine. He's a tramp."

"And what are you?"

"Something like one now, sir, but I wasn't always."

"Is the infant there your sister?"

"She's only my sister the big way: God made her."

"Why is she with you then?"

"Someone threw her in a water barrel, and I heard the splash, and went and got her out."

"Why did you not take her to the police?"

"I never thought of that. It was all I could do to keep her alive. I couldn't have done it if we hadn't got into the house."

"How long ago was that?"

"Nearly a month, sir."

"And you've kept her there ever since?"

"Yes, sir—as well as I could. I had only sixpence a day."

"And what's the boy's name?"

"Tommy, sir. I don't know any other."

"Nice respectable company you keep for one who has evidently been well brought up!"

"Baby's quite respectable, sir! And Tommy, if I didn't keep him, would steal. I'm teaching him not to steal."

"Who attends the baby?"

"I do, sir. When I'm away, Tommy and Abdiel take care of her."

"Abdiel! Who on earth is that?" asked the magistrate, looking around for some fourth member of the family.

"He's not on earth, sir. He's in heaven—the good angel, you know, sir, that left Satan and came back again to God."

"You must take him to the county asylum, James!" said the magistrate, turning to the tall policeman.

"Oh, he's all right, sir!" said James.

"Please, sir," interrupted Clare eagerly, "I didn't mean the dog was in heaven yet. I meant the angel I named him after!"

"They *had* a little dog with them, sir!"

"Yes, Abdiel," said Clare. "He wanted to be a prisoner too, but they wouldn't let him. He followed me home because he hadn't anybody to love. He don't have much to eat, but he's content."

"Have you work of any sort?"

"I had till yesterday, sir, at Mr. Maidstone's shop."

"What wages did you earn?"

"Sixpence a day."

"And all three of you live on that?"

"Yes, all four of us, sir."

"What do you do at the shop?"

"Please, your worship," interposed policeman James, "he was sent about his business yesterday."

"Yes," rejoined Clare, who did not understand the phrase. "I was sent with a lady to carry her bandbox to the station."

"And when you came back, you was turned away, wasn't you?" James asked.

"Yes, sir."

"What had you done?" asked the magistrate.

"I don't quite know, sir."

"Do you expect me to believe that?"

"Of course I do, sir."

"Why?"

"Because it is true."

"How am I to believe that?"

"I don't know, sir. I only know I've got to speak the truth. It's the person who hears it that's got to believe it, ain't it, sir?"

"You've got to prove it."

"I don't think so, sir. I was only told I must speak the truth—I never was told I must prove what it said. I've been several times disbelieved by people who did not know me."

"Never by people who did know you?"

"I think not, sir. I never was doubted by the people at home."

"Ah! You could not read what they were thinking!"

"Were you not believed when you were at home, sir?"

The magistrate doubted Clare because when he had been a boy, he did not always tell the truth—and he had suffered severely. He was annoyed, therefore, at Clare's question. He had a strong desire to shame him.

"I remand the prisoner for more evidence. Take the children to the workhouse," he said.

Tommy gave a sudden howl. He had heard tales about the workhouse.

"The baby is mine!" pleaded Clare.

"Are you the father of it?" the big policeman asked.

"Yes, I think so. I saved her life. She would have drowned if I hadn't looked for her when I heard the splash!" reasoned Clare, his face drawn with grief and the struggle to keep from crying.

"She's not yours," said the magistrate. "She belongs to the

parish. Take her away, James."

The big policeman came up to take her. Clare asked, "Will the parish be good to her?"

"Much better than you."

"Will you let me go and see her?" he asked with a sob.

"You can't go anywhere till you're out of this," answered the big policeman, and gently took the baby from him.

"And when will that be, please?" asked Clare, with his empty arms still held out.

"That depends on his worship there."

"Hold your tongue, James," said the magistrate. "Take the boy away, John."

"Please, sir, where am I going?" Clare asked.

"To prison till we find out about you."

"Please, sir, I didn't mean to steal her. I didn't know the parish wanted her!"

"Take the boy away, I tell you!" cried the magistrate angrily. "His tongue goes like the hopper of a mill!"

James, carrying the baby on one arm, was already pushing Tommy before him by the neck. Tommy howled, and rubbed his red eyes, but did not resist.

John tightened his grasp on Clare's arm, and hurried him away in another direction.

When the big policemen issued with his charge, there was Abdiel hovering about. When he spied Tommy, he rushed at him. Tommy gave him a kick that rolled him over.

"Don't want *you*, you mangy beast!" he said, and tried to kick him again.

Abdiel turned to the entrance and lay down. He knew that Clare had gone in with the others and that he was within still.

The police asked about Clare at Mr. Maidstone's shop. Reasons for Clare's dismissal involved no accusation. There was therefore nothing to the discredit of the boy, except living in the neglected house. After three days, Clare was set free from prison.

CHAPTER FOURTEEN
Away

The moment Clare stepped out of the prison door, he met Abdiel, clinging to him with his forelegs, and wagging his tail as if he would shake it off for gladness!

Clare could not go back to the shop; he could not go back to the house; he could not stop in town. Where was he to go? There was no one place for him better than another! But they would let him see the baby before he went, and off he set to the workhouse, with Abdiel following at his heel.

At the workhouse Clare asked to see the matron. She, knowing the story of the baby, wanted to see Clare, and was pleased with his manners and looks. She took him to the room where the babies were, telling him he must prove the baby was his by picking her out. Although the baby was decently clothed and had already improved in appearance, Clare knew her the moment he saw her on the lap of an old woman.

"Let me take her," said Clare modestly, holding out his hands for the baby.

She gave him the baby, and watched him with the eye of a seeress*—she had a wonderful insight into character, and that is one of the roots of prophecy. "You are a good and true lad," she said at length, "and a hard success lies before you. I don't know what you will come to, but if you come to anything but good, you will be terribly to blame."

"I will try to be good, ma'am," said Clare simply. "But I wish I knew what they put me in prison for!"

"What, indeed, my lamb!" she returned, and her eyes flashed with indignation under the cornice of her white hair.

91

"They'll be put in prison one day themselves!"

"Oh, I don't mind!" said Clare. "I don't want them to be punished. You see, I'm only waiting."

"What are you waiting for, sonny?" asked the old woman.

"I don't exactly know—but I'm always waiting for something."

"The something will come, child. You will have what you want! Only go on as you're doing, and you'll be a great man one day."

"I don't want to be a great man," answered Clare. "I'm only waiting till what is coming does come."

The woman seemed lost in thought. Clare handled the baby gently in his arms, and talked lovingly to her. "Well," said the old woman, raising her eyes with a look of reverence in them, "I can't help you. I've got no money, but—"

"I've got plenty of money, ma'am," interrupted Clare. "I've got a whole shilling in my pocket!"

"Bless the holy innocent!" murmured the woman. "Well, I can only promise you—that as long as I live, the baby won't forget you."

Here the matron came up, and told Clare to go—but if he came back any day after a month, he would see the baby again.

"Thank you, ma'am," replied Clare. "Keep her a good baby, please. I will come for her one day."

So Clare went once more into the street and stood on the pavement with Abdiel, not knowing which way to turn. In a moment it occurred to him that, having come in at one end of town, he should go out at the other. Abdiel followed him.

Clare saw that the dog was famished. He stopped at a butcher's and bought him a scrap of meat for a penny. Then he had elevenpence with which to begin the world afresh, and was not hungry.

Out on the highway they went, on a perfect English summer day, with all the world before them. They trudged on for some time without speaking. Ready to do anything,

Clare asked for work at every farm they came to. But he was not successful.

But now and then some tender-hearted woman would perceive the boy's hunger and offer him food. Never doubting what came to one was for both, Clare always gave the first share of it to Abdiel.

For many days they tramped along. Clare grew more hopeless of getting work, but not more doubtful that everything was right. For he knew nothing he had done had brought these things upon him. At the worst pinch of hunger and cold, he never fell into despair.

CHAPTER FIFTEEN

The Caravans and the Bull

Passing one day from a country road into the highway, Clare came upon a travelling menagerie. The front part of the procession had already gone by, and an elephant was passing at the moment, pulling a caravan of feline creatures behind him. A world of delight woke in Clare's heart. He had never seen an elephant.

At the end of the procession came a bear, shuffling along uncomfortably. "What a life it would be," Clare thought, "to have all these creatures to make happy!"

Behind the bear, came a stoutish, good-tempered looking man in a small cart pulled by a pony. He was the earthly owner of the caged animals. The moment he had passed, Clare fell in behind as one of the procession. When he had followed it thus for a mile or two, he saw that they were coming near a town. Before reaching it, they arrived at a spot where the hedges receded from the road, and there the long line came to a halt.

The menagerie was to be exhibited the next day in the town they were approaching. They made this stop to prepare their entrance. To let a part of their treasure be seen was the best way to rouse desire after what was yet hidden: therefore they were going to take out an animal or two to walk in the parade. Clare sat down at a little distance, and wondered what was coming next.

The men disliked having their proceedings watched by anybody—but happily for Clare, it was the master himself who came up to him. Clare rose and took off his cap.

"What are you hanging about here for?" he asked rudely.

"I beg your pardon, sir," he said. "I did not understand you wished to be alone. I never thought you would mind me. Will it be far enough if I go just out of sight, for I am very tired! It is pleasant, besides, to know there are friends near."

The man recognized in Clare the modes and speech of a gentleman.

"Never mind," he said. "I see you're after no mischief!" and with that walked away, leaving Clare to do as he pleased.

Hungry and sleepy, Clare sat on the grass by the roadside. The next moment he was on his feet, startled by a terrible noise. The lion had opened his great jaws, and had sent from his throat a huge blast—half roar, half howl.

Then Clare heard a roar of a different kind. Down the road, he saw a cloud of dust and a confused struggle between two men, each at the end of a rope, and an animal attached to the ropes by a ring in his nose. It was a bull, bounding this way and that, doing his best to break away.

Clare could see the bloody foam drip from the poor beast's nostrils. When about fifty yards away, the bull twisted the rope from the hands of one man. The man fell on his back, the other dropped his rope and fled, and the bull came scouring down the highway.

A second roar of muffled thunder issued from the lion. The bull made a sudden stop. Then down went his head, and like a black flash, he charged one of the caravans. He had taken the hungry lion's roar for a challenge to combat.

The men busy about the caravans and wagons saw him coming, and bolted for refuge. The same moment, the bull's head cracked against the near hind wheel of the caravan in whose shafts stood the elephant. The bull had not caught sight of the elephant, or he would doubtless have gone for him. In that caravan was the lion, who answered the blow of the bull's head with a thunderous roar. It roused every creature in the menagerie. Out burst a tornado of terrific sound—the roaring and yelling of lion, tiger, and leopard, the laughter of hyenas, the howling of jackal, and the snarling of bear, mingled with the cries of monkeys and parrots.

By this time the men had caught up what weapons were at hand, and rushed to repel the bull. But then the enraged beast entangled his horns in the spokes and rim of the wheel.

While the master hesitated, Clare came running up with Abdiel at his heels. The moment Clare saw how the bull's horns were mixed up with the spokes of the wheel, he thought, *That was old Nimrod's way!* The men stood about the bull, as he struggled with his horns, and heaved and tore at the wheel to get them out of it.

Up rushed a fellow, white with rage. It was one of two men from whom Nimrod had broken. He held a pitchfork, which he proceeded to level. Clare flung his weight against the men, threw up his fork, shoved him aside, and got close to the maddened animal. With instinctive, unconscious authority, he held up his hand to the little crowd.

"Leave him alone!" he cried. "I know him! I can manage him! He is an old friend of mine."

They saw that the bull was already still—the animal had recognized the boy's voice!

"Nimrod!" Clare whispered, laying a hand on one of the creature's horns, and his cheek against his neck. "I'm going to get your horns out," murmured Clare, and laid hold of the other with a firm grasp.

By the horns Clare turned the bull's head one way, then another. In a moment more he would have them clear, for one of them was already free. Holding on the latter, Clare turned to the bystanders. "You mustn't touch him," he said, "or I won't answer for him. And you mustn't let either of those men there interfere with him or me. They let him go because they couldn't manage him."

Clare gently released the other horn, but kept his hold of the first, moving Nimrod's head by it, this way and that. A moment more and he turned his face to the crowd, which had scattered a little. Clare still made the bull feel his hand on his horn, and kept speaking to him gently and lovingly.

Nimrod eyed his enemies with triumph. Clare began to untie the ropes from the ring in Nimrod's nose, but the man with the pitchfork interfered.

"That wonnot do!" he said, and laid his hand on Clare's arm. "Would you send him ramping over the country without a hold on him?"

"It wasn't much good when you had a hold on him, was it now?" returned the boy. "Where do you want to take him?"

"That's my business," answered the man sulkily.

"I fancy you'll find it's mine!" returned Clare. "But there he is! Take him."

The man hesitated.

"Then let me manage him," said Clare.

While he was untying the first of the ropes from the animal's bleeding nostrils, Clare's fingers stopped, his eyes grew dim, and he fell senseless at the bull's feet.

"Don't tell Nimrod!" he murmured as he fell.

"Oh, that explains it!" cried the man with pitchfork to his mate. "He knows the cursed brute!" But the explanation lay in the bull's knowing Clare, not in Clare's knowing the bull.

They rushed to hold the ropes. Nimrod stood motionless, looking down on his friend, now and then snuffing at the pale face, which Abdiel kept licking continuously.

The men of the caravan, admiring both Clare's influence over the animal and his management of him, grateful also for what he had done for them, hurried to help him. When they had gotten him to take a little brandy, he sat up with a weak smile, but soon fell sideways on his elbow and to the ground again.

"It's nothing," he murmured. "I'm only rather hungry."

"Poor boy!" said a woman who had followed her brandy from the house-caravan, afraid it might disappear in unauthorized directions. "When did you have your last meal?"

"I had a piece of bread yesterday afternoon, ma'am," Clare explained. "But I believe it was the gladness of seeing an old friend again that made me faint."

"Where's your friend?" she asked, looking around.

"There he is!" answered Clare, putting up his hand and stroking Nimrod's nose.

"Can you get up now?" asked the woman. "I want you to come into the house and have a good square meal."

"Would you be so kind, ma'am, as to let me have a bit of bread here? Nimrod would not like me to leave him. He loves me, ma'am, and if I went away, he might be troublesome."

Clare's eyes closed again. The woman made haste to get him a basin of broth, which he took eagerly. Before he tasted it, however, he set it on the ground, broke in half the great piece of bread she had brought with it, and gave the larger part to his dog. Then he ate the rest with his broth.

"You'd better take your bull away," the woman said to the two men.

They were silent, evidently not ready for another tussle.

"You'd better be going," she said again. "If anything should happen with that animal of yours, and one of ours was to get loose, the devil would be to pay, and who'd do it?"

"They'd better wait for me, ma'am," said Clare, rising. "I'm ready! They won't tell me where they want to take him, but it's all one, so long as I'm with him. He's my friend—ain't you, Nimrod? We'll go together."

While he spoke, he untied the ropes from the ring in the bull's nose. Gathering them up, he handed them politely to one of the men. The next moment he sprang upon the bull's back, and leaning forward, stroked his horns and neck.

"Give me the dog, please," he said.

The owner of the menagerie himself did as Clare requested. All stood and stared, half expecting to see him flung from the creature's back and trampled under his hooves. But Nimrod was far from wishing to unseat his friend, who with hands and legs began to guide him toward the road.

"Are you going that way?" Clare asked, pointing. The men answered him with a nod.

"Don't go with those men," said the woman, coming up to

the side of the bull, and speaking in a low voice. "I don't like the look of them."

"Nimrod will be on my side, ma'am," answered Clare. "They would never have got him home without me. They don't understand their fellow-creatures."

"I'm afraid you understand your fellow-creatures, as you call them, better than you do your own kind!"

"I think they are my own kind, ma'am. That is how they know me and do what I want them to do."

"Stay with us," said the woman coaxingly, still speaking low. "You'll have plenty of your fellow-creatures about you then!"

"Thank you, ma'am," answered Clare. "But I couldn't leave poor Nimrod to do those men mischief, and be killed for it!"

Here the master of the menagerie came up. He had himself been thinking the boy would be a great acquisition, and guessed what his wife was trying to do. But he was afraid she might promise too much for services that ought to be had cheap.

"I won't feel safe till that bull of yours is a mile off!" he said.

"Come along, Nimrod!" answered Clare, always ready with the responsive deed.

Away went Nimrod, gentle as a lamb, and the two men followed at their ease. No sooner was Nimrod on the road, however, than he began to quicken his pace. Within a minute or so he was trotting swiftly along. The men ran panting and shouting behind. The more they shouted, the faster Nimrod went. Before long, he was out of their sight, though Clare could hear them cursing and calling for a time.

Clare hesitated to stop Nimrod, but the bull seemed to have made up his mind that he had obeyed enough for one day. He did not heed a word Clare said to him, but kept on and on at a swinging trot. For a few miles, Nimrod was content with the highway. But all at once he turned at right angles in the middle of the road, cleared the skirting fence like a hunter, and took a beeline across the fields. On and on he went, over hedge after hedge, through field after field, until Clare began to wonder where they were going. Then a strange feeling gradually came over him. Surely at some time or other he had seen the meadow he was crossing!

It was plain why Nimrod was so obstinate. The dear old fellow was carrying Clare back to where they had been together so many happy days! They were near Mr. Goodenough's farm, and heading straight for it! Delight filled Clare's heart at the thought of seeing once more the places where his father and mother seemed yet to live.

They were soon upon the farm. Nimrod was making for his old stable. He was weary now, and breathing heavily, though not at all spent.

When they reached Nimrod's door, they found it closed; and Clare, stiff enough by this time, slipped off to open it. Nimrod began to paw the stones, and blow angry puffs from his wounded nose. When Clare got the door open, he saw another bull in Nimrod's stall! The roar that simultaneously burst from each was ferocious, and down went Nimrod's head to charge.

It was a terrible moment for Clare: the new bull was tied by ropes fastened around his head; unable to turn his head toward his adversary, he would be gored to death in a moment! Clare could not let Nimrod be guilty of such unfairness! He all but jumped on Nimrod's horns, making him yield just ground enough to shut the door. With his back to it, Clare stood facing Nimrod and talking to him, all the while hearing the bull inside struggling to get free.

Before he could get Nimrod away, the bellowing brought out Farmer Goodenough. "What's got the brute?" he cried on the threshold, but instantly began to run, for he saw through the gathering darkness a darker shape he knew, roaring and pawing at the door of his old quarters, and a boy standing between him and it. He understood at once that Nimrod had broken loose and come back. But when he came nearer he recognized Clare.

"Clare!" he stammered.

"Yes, sir," returned Clare, and laid hold of Nimrod's horn. The animal yielded, and turned away with him.

The farmer came nearer, and put his arm round the boy's neck. The boy rubbed his cheek against the arm.

"I'm sorry I struck you, Clare!" faltered the big man.

"Oh, never mind, sir! That was long ago!" answered the boy.

"Tell me how you've been getting on."

"Pretty well, sir! But I want to tell you first how it is I'm here with Nimrod. Only it would be better to put him somewhere before I begin."

"It would," agreed the farmer. Between them, with the enticements of a pail of water and some fresh-cut grass, they got Nimrod into a shed, where they hoped he would forget about the other bull and, with the soothing help of his supper, go to sleep.

Then Clare told his story. If Mr. Goodenough had not known him for a boy that would not lie, he would not have believed it.

"Come, Abdiel!" said Clare, the moment he ended his story, for he was ready to leave.

"Won't you have something to eat after your long ride?" the farmer asked.

Clare looked down at his clothes and laughed. The farmer knew what he meant, and did not ask him into the house.

"Then if you must go, I'm glad for the opportunity to pay you the wages I owe you," said the farmer, putting his hand in his pocket.

"You gave me my food! That was all I was worth!" protested Clare.

"You were worth more than that. I knew the difference when I had another boy in your place. I wish I had you again. But it wouldn't do, you know," he added hastily.

With that he pulled a sovereign* from his pocket and held it out to Clare. It seemed an enormous wealth to the boy. He could not help holding out his hand, but he was ashamed to open it.

"It's too much!" he protested, looking at the sovereign almost in fear. "I never had so much money in my life!"

"You earned it well," said the farmer magnanimously.

The moral cramp forsook Clare's hand. He took the money with a hearty, "Thank you, sir," and put it in his pocket.

"Where are you going?" asked the farmer.

Clare mentioned the small town in whose neighborhood he had left the caravans, and said he thought the people of the menagerie would like him to help them with the beasts. The farmer shook his head.

"It's not a respectable occupation!" he remarked.

Clare did not understand him. "Do they cheat?" he asked.

"No, I don't suppose they cheat worse than anybody else. But it ain't respectable."

Clare thought everything honest was honorable. When people said otherwise, he did not understand.

Clare made no attempt to argue the question with the farmer. He asked him the nearest way to town, and went—quickly when he heard Mrs. Goodenough calling her husband to supper.

CHAPTER SIXTEEN
A Rolling Home

Clare trudged along merrily, and Abdiel shared his joy. They had to sleep outside nevertheless—for by this time Clare knew that a boy, especially a boy in rags, must mind whom he asks to change a sovereign. In the lee of a haymow, on a little loose hay, Clare and Abdiel slept.

There was not much temptation to lie around long after waking, and the companions were early on their way. It was night when they entered the town. They were already weary when the far sounds of the brass band of the menagerie first entered their ears. Its notes were just dying to their close, when Clare climbed the steps leading to the platform where the musicians stood. Abdiel crept after him.

At a table on the platform sat the mistress, ready to receive the money of those who entered. Clare laid his sovereign before her. She took it up but she looked at it doubtfully. She threw it on her table. It would not ring. She bit it with her white teeth, and looked at it again, and then gave a glance at the person who offered it. Her dull lamp flickered in the puffs of the night-wind, and she did not recognize Clare.

"Won't pass," she said with decision. "Ain't you got sixpence?"

"No, ma'am," answered Clare. "I haven't had sixpence for many a day."

The moment he spoke, the woman looked him sharply in the face and knew him. "Drat my stupid eyes!" she said fervently. "That I shouldn't ha' known you! Walk in, go where you please. Where did you get that sovereign?"

"From Farmer Goodenough."

"Good enough, I hope, not to take advantage of you! Was it for taking home the bull?"

"No, ma'am. I didn't take the bull home. The bull took me to the old home where we used to be together."

"Well, never mind now. Go in, or the show'll be over. Look after your dog, though. He mustn't go in."

"I'll send him right outside, if you wish it, ma'am."

"I do—but will he stay out?"

"He will, ma'am."

Clare took up Abdiel, set him at the top of the steps, and told him to go down and wait. Abdiel hopped down, turned in under the steps, and deposited himself there.

A strange smell was in Clare's nostrils, and as he went down the steps inside, it grew stronger. He wondered why these animals should smell different from domestic animals. He was soon in the midst of a vision attractive to all boys, but which few had ever looked upon with such intelligent wonder as he; for Clare had read and reread every book about animals he could find. He had a great power too for remembering what he read. What with pictures and descriptions he remembered, as he looked around him, he seemed to know every animal he saw.

Clare's eyes rested on the tenant of one of the cages, a big blackish animal with a big ring in his nose. To the ring was fastened a strong chain, and the chain was bolted down to the metal floor of the cage. The chain was so short that it held the poor creature's head within about a foot of the floor. He could not lift it higher, or move it farther on either side, but he kept moving it constantly. He was a terrible brute, a big grizzly bear, ugly to repulsiveness.

"Poor fellow!" said Clare. "How can he be good-tempered with that torturing ring and chain!"

The boy turned aside with a quivering heart—sore for the grizzly's nose, and sorer still for the grizzly himself that he was so unfriendly.

Right opposite, a creature of a far differing disposition

seemed casting defiance to all the ills of life. The creature kept bounding from side to side in his cage, agile and frolicsome as a kitten. He was yellowish like a lion, but had no mane.

Clare was taken with the frolicsome creature. As he gazed and sympathized, there awoke within him that strange consciousness of being on the point of remembering something. It was not a memory that came, but a memory of a memory, the shadow of a memory gone—a sense of having once known something. It gave another aspect to the blessed creature before him. The creature and he himself seemed for a moment to belong together to another time. Could he have seen such an animal before? Clare did not think so! He could never have visited a menagerie and forgotten it! He could recognize the lion and the tiger and the leopard, although he seemed to know he had never seen any of them. But he did not know this animal.

While Clare stood looking at the one creature, he grew tired. He decided to search for some field where he could sleep. He went out onto the deserted platform, and down the steps. Abdiel was already at the foot when he reached it, wagging his weary little tail. They lay down under one of the wagons and fell asleep.

When Clare next looked up, he saw nothing between him and the sky. They had dragged the caravan from above him, and he had not moved. Abdiel indeed woke at the first pull, but had lain as still as a mouse.

Clare saw the sky, but he saw something else over him— the face of Mrs. Halliwell, the mistress of the menagerie.

Clare jumped up, saying, "Good morning, ma'am!" He was only half awake, and staggered with sleep.

"My poor boy!" answered the woman. "I sent you to sleep on the cold earth, with a sovereign of your own in my pocket! I made sure you would come and ask me for it! You're too innocent to go about the world without a mother!"

"But, ma'am, you know I couldn't have offered it to anybody," said Clare. "It wasn't good! Besides, before I knew that," he went on, finding she did not reply, "there was nobody but you I dared offer it to: they would have said I stole it—because I'm so shabby!" he added, looking down at his rags.

Getting the better of her feelings for a moment, she said, "It was all my fault! The sovereign is a good one—it's only cracked! I ought to have known, and changed it for you. Then all would have been well!"

"I'm so glad!" said Clare. "I was sure Mr. Goodenough thought the sovereign all right when he gave it to me! Were you ever disappointed in a sovereign, ma'am?"

"I been oftener disappointed in them as owed 'em!" she answered. "But to think o'me snug in bed, an' you sleeping' out i' the dark night! I couldn't bear the thought of it!"

"Don't let it trouble you, ma'am. We're used to it."

"Then you oughtn't to be! And, please God, you shall be no more! Come along and have your breakfast."

"Please, ma'am, may Abdiel come too?"

"Of course! Your dog's well-behaved. Still, he must learn not to come in sight o' the animals."

"He will learn, ma'am! Abdiel, lie down, and don't come till I call you." At the word, the dog dropped, and lay.

The house-caravan stood a little way off. They ascended its steps behind, and entered an enchanting little room. It had muslin curtains on the windows, and a small stove in which you could see the bright red coals. On the stove stood a coffeepot and a covered dish. How nice and warm the place felt after the nearly shelterless night!

The breakfast-things were still on the table. Mr. Halliwell had eaten his breakfast, but Mrs. Halliwell would not eat until she had found the boy. She had worried about him all night.

They sat down to breakfast, and the good woman was soon sure that the boy was a gentleman. "Call your dog now," she said, "an' let's see if he'll come!"

"May I whistle, ma'am?"

"Why not! But will he hear you?"

"He has very sharp ears, ma'am."

Clare gave a low, peculiar whistle. In a second or two, they heard an anxious little whine at the door, and there stood Abdiel. The woman caught him and held him to her bosom.

"You blessed little thing!" she said.

Clare heard and felt the horses hitched to the wagon, but his hostess did not rise, and he too went on with his breakfast. When they were in motion, it was not so easy to eat nicely, but Clare managed. By the time he had finished, they had left the town behind them. Nothing had been said about his going with them; she had taken that for granted. Clare thought that he and Abdiel ought to get out and walk, instead of burdening the poor horses with their weight. But when he said so to Mrs. Halliwell, she told him she must have a little talk with him first, and formally proposed that he should enter their service, and do whatever he was fit for in the menagerie.

"You're not frightened of the beasts are you?" she said.

"Oh no, ma'am—I love them!" answered Clare. "But are you sure Mr. Halliwell thinks I could be of use?"

"Don't you think you could?" she asked.

"I know I could, ma'am, but I would not like him to take me just because he feels sorry for me!"

"No, no! He saw the way you managed that bull—a far more unreasonable creature than any we have to deal with!"

"Ah! You don't know Nimrod, ma'am!"

"I don't, a' I don't want to! Such wild animals ought to be put in caravans!" she added, with a laugh.

"Well, ma'am," said Clare, "if you and Mr. Halliwell agree, nothing would please me so much as to serve you and the beasts. But I should like to be sure about it, for where husband and wife are not of one mind—well, it is uncomfortable!"

Thereupon he told her how he had stood with the farmer and his wife, and from that she led him on through his whole story—accompanied with tears on Clare's part. In her heart Mrs. Halliwell rejoiced that the boy's sufferings would now be at an end—and thereafter she became his third mother.

The next time they stopped, she made her husband come into the caravan and arrange everything. When both her husband and the boy would have left his wages undetermined, she would not hear of it, but insisted that so much a week should be fixed at once to begin with. She had no doubt that her husband would soon be ready to raise Clare's wages. But the boy had to have his food and five shillings a week now, and Mr. Halliwell had to advance money to get Clare decent clothes.

At the next town Clare's new mother saw him dressed to their mutual satisfaction. She would have his holiday clothes better than his present part in life required, and she would not let his sovereign go toward paying for them: that she would keep in case he might want it!

Clare had plenty to do. Every morning he took his share in cleaning out the cages, and in setting water for the beasts, and food for the birds and such other creatures as took it when they pleased. At the proper intervals he fed as many as he might of those animals that had stated times for their meals, and found the advantage of this in its facilitating his friendly approaches to them. He helped with the horses also, with whose harness and ways he was already familiar. Soon he was known as a friend by every civilized animal in and about the caravans.

CHAPTER SEVENTEEN
Glum Gunn

Clare had but one enemy, Glum Gunn. For Gunn was so different from Clare that he disliked the boy the moment he saw him, and it took but a day to ripen his dislike into hatred. Unhappily for Clare, Gunn was of consequence in the menagerie, for he had money invested in it.

Glum Gunn was half brother to Mr. Halliwell, but most unlike him. He was the terror of the men beneath him, heeding no man but his brother—and him only because he knew he would stand no nonsense. To his sister-in-law, Gunn was civil: she was his brother's wife, and his brother was proud of her.

Clare had no suspicion that Gunn hated him. It took him days indeed to discover that Gunn did not love him—even though the man's angry eyes kept constantly following him.

It was natural that such a man should also be cruel. He had no liking for any of the animals, regarding them only as property. Yet he prided himself that he had a great influence as well as power over them, a superiority that made him their lord. By the terror of his whip, and by means far worse, he compelled their obedience. The grizzly was the only animal he never bothered.

From the beginning he received Clare's, "Good-morning, sir," with a silent stare. The boy, thinking he did not like to be so greeted, gave up the salutation. This roused Gunn's anger and increased his hate.

Gunn saw that Clare never resented anything. He learned that the boy never carried tales to his sister-in-law, of which he took advantage, and set about making life bitter for Clare.

Gunn put Clare to the dirtiest work only to find that it did not trouble him: the boy was a rare gentleman—unwilling that another should have more so that he might have less of the disagreeable. For no man has the right to require of another the thing he would think degrading to himself.

The boy had to take his turn in acting as showman to the gazing crowd, and by and by the part fell to him the most often. Each had his own way of filling the office. One would repeat his information like a lesson in which he was not interested. Another made himself the clown of the exhibition, and joked as much and as well as he could. Gunn delighted in telling as many lies as he dared: he must not be suspected of making fools of his audience! But Clare knew far more than any of the others about the creatures from the books he had read. By watching the animals because he loved them, Clare had already noticed things none of the others had observed, and was quickly learning more. He talked to the spectators out of his own sincere and warm interest, telling them about things he had read and things he had discovered himself. Group after group of simple country people would listen intently as the boy led them around, eager after every word—and this success was noted with an evil eye by Glum Gunn.

By this time all the beasts with any friendliness in them had for Clare a little more than their usual amount of that feeling. But there was one with whom a real friendship had begun and had grown. Clare's new friend was the puma, or cougar, a relation to the jaguar. But while the jaguar is as wicked a beast as the tiger, the puma possesses, in relation to man, far more than the generosity of the lion. A distinctive characteristic of the puma is his love for the human being—a persistent, devoted, and long-suffering love.

The caravan came to a town where they exhibited every day for a week, and there it was that the friendship of Clare and the puma reached its perfection. One night the boy could not sleep, and went down among the cages to see how his fellow-creatures were doing. There was just light enough from a small moon to show the dim outlines of the cages, and the motion without the form of any moving animal. The puma, in his solitary yet joyous gymnastics, was celebrating the rites of freedom according to his custom.

Clare went to him and began to stroke him on the face and nose, whereupon the puma began to lick the boy's hand with his dry rough tongue. The boy had his arm between the bars of the cage, and his face pressed close against them, when suddenly the puma rubbed his face against Clare's.

Clare pulled aside the bolt of the cage door and got in beside the puma. The creature's gladness was even greater than if he had found a friend of his own kind. Noses and cheeks and heads were rubbed together, and hands stroked and scratched. Then they played a long time, the puma jumping over Clare, and Clare tumbling over the puma. Finally, the boy fell fast asleep, and in the morning found the puma's head lying across his body, wide awake but motionless, as if guarding him. Nobody was awake, so Clare crept quietly from the cage and went to his own bed.

The next night, as soon as the place was quiet, Clare went down and had another game with the puma. Before their sport was over, he had begun to teach him some of the tricks he had taught Abdiel.

The same thing took place as often as possible for some weeks, and Clare came to have as much confidence, in so far at least as good intention was concerned, in the puma as in Abdiel. If only he could have let him out of the cage! But not being certain how the puma would behave or if he could then control him, he felt had had no right to release him.

Now and then Clare would fall asleep in the cage, whereupon the puma would always lie down close beside him. On one such occasion, Clare jumped to his feet half-awake, roused by a terrific fear. Right up on end stood the cougar, flattening his front against the bars of the cage, which he clawed furious, snarling and spitting and yelling. Clatter, clatter, went his great feet on the iron, as he tore now at this bar, now at that, to get at something out in the dim open space. It was too dark for Clare to see what it was that infuriated him, but he could hear something. Woven into the mad noise of the wild creature, the boy heard the modest whimper of Abdiel.

Clare had taken time to make Abdiel understand that he was not to intrude where his presence was not desired. The animal show was not for him, and Clare thought the dog had learned perfectly that he was never to bother the animals.

When Clare left Abdiel, he thought he had carefully shut him into a small cage he used on such occasions. But the boy had not been careful enough, and Abdiel had interpreted the unfastened door as a sign that he might follow his master. As soon as Clare saw what the problem was, he slipped out of the puma's cage and picked up the obnoxious offender. He sped the dog back to his cage and gave him a serious talking to.

The puma was quiet the moment Abdiel was out of his sight. But Gunn, wakened by the roaring, came flying toward the cages with his whip. He rushed across the area, jumped into the cage of the puma, and began lashing him with his whip. The beast whimpered and wept.

Clare heard the changed cry of his friend, and came swooping like the guardian angel he was. He saw the patient creature on his haunches like a dog, accepting Gunn's brutality without an attempt to escape it—except by dodging any blows toward his head. Clare bounded to the cage, wild with anger and pity. But Gunn stood with his back against the door of it.

"O sir! Sir!" he cried, in a voice full of tears. "It was all my fault! Abby came to look for me!"

"Do you tell me, you rascal, that you were down among the animals when I thought you was in your bed?"

"Yes, sir, I was. I didn't know there was any harm. I wasn't doing anything wrong."

"Hold your jaw! What was you doing?"

"I was only in the cage with the puma."

"You was! You have the impudence to tell me that to my

face! I'll teach you, you milk-pudding! To go corrupting the animals and making them not worth their salt!"

Gunn swung himself out of the cage door in a fury, but Clare, with his friend in danger, would not run. The man seized him by the collar, and began to lash him as he had been lashing the puma.

With the first lash came a tearing screech from the puma, as he flung himself in fury upon the door of his cage. Gunn in his wrath with Clare had forgotten to bolt it. The puma pulled it open with his claws, and like a huge shell for a mortar, shot himself at Gunn. Down he went.

For one moment the puma stood over him, swinging his tail in great sweeps, and looking at him. Then before Clare could lay hold of the animal, the puma turned a scornful back upon his enemy. He walked away with a slow, careless stride, leaped into his cage, and lay down.

The thing happened so fast that Clare did not see him touch the man with his paw, and thought the puma had only thrown Gunn down with his weight. The beast, however, had not left the brute without the lesson he needed: he had given him just one little pat on the side of the head.

Gunn rose staggering. The skin and something more was torn down his cheek from the temple almost to the chin, and the blood was streaming. Clare rushed to help him, but Gunn flung him aside, muttering with an oath, "I'll make you pay for this!" and went out, holding his head with both hands.

Clare went and shut the bolt of the cage. The puma sprang up, expecting the boy to play with him. But Clare bade him good-night with a kiss through the bars

Glum Gunn stayed in bed for more than a week. When at last he reappeared, he was not beautiful to look upon. Though he had been treated by the best doctor in the town, for the rest of his evil earthly days he bore an ugly scar. Neither his heart nor his temper were the better for his well-deserved punishment.

Mrs. Halliwell asked Clare about the whole thing. Her

lengthy questioning ended with a partial discovery of Gunn's behavior toward Clare, whom she loved even more since he had been so silent concerning it. She stood perturbed. One moment her face flushed with anger, the next turned pale with apprehension. She bit her lip, and the tears came in her eyes.

"Never mind, Mother," Clare said, who saw no reason for such emotion. "I'm not afraid of him."

"I know *you're* not," she answered, "but that don't make me any less afraid for you. He's a bad man, that brother-in-law of mine! I fear he'll do something terrible to you. I'm afraid I did wrong in bringing you with us. I should have done what I could for you without taking you along. We can't get rid of Gunn because he's got money in the business. Not that he's part owner—I don't mean that! If we'd got the money handy, we'd pay him off at once!"

"I don't care about myself," said Clare. "I don't mean I like to be kicked, but it don't make me miserable. What I can't bear is to see him being cruel to the beasts. I love the beasts, Mother—even old Grizzly—but Mr. Gunn don't meddle much with him!"

"He respects his own ugly sort!" laughed Mrs. Halliwell.

For a while it was plain to the boy that Mr. Halliwell kept an eye on his brother, and on him and the puma. On one occasion he told the assembled staff that he would have no tyranny: everyone knew there was only one tyrant among them. Gunn saw that his brother was awake and watching: it was a check on his conduct, but he hated Clare even worse. For the puma, Gunn was afraid of him now and went no more into his cage.

With the rest of the men Clare was a favorite. He was helpful and they could always depend on him. Abdiel shared in the favor shown his master. They said the dog was no beauty, and had not a hair of breeding, but he was almost a human creature.

CHAPTER EIGHTEEN
Abdiel's Peril

They had opened the menagerie in a certain large town. It was the evening exhibition, and Clare was acting as showman. He pointed his wand to the different animals and told what he thought would most interest his hearers.

Just then another attendant came up behind him and whispered that Glum Gunn had gotten hold of Abdiel, and was going to harm the dog. Clare instantly gave him his wand, and bolted through the crowd. He scolded himself for shutting the dog up in his cage. If he had not been shut up, Gunn would not have gotten hold of him.

When Clare reached the top of the steps, there was Gunn on the platform, addressing the crowd. It was plain to the boy that he had been drinking. He had the poor dog by the scruff of the neck, and was holding him out at arm's length. Abdiel had his hind legs drawn up, his tail tucked in tight between them, and his backbone curved into a half circle. In this uncomfortable plight, the tyrant was making a burlesque speech about him.

"Here you see, ladies and gentlemen," he said, "one of the most extraordinary productions of the vegetable kingdom. It is not unnatural that you should dispute my assertion. But when I have the honor of leaving you to your astonishment, I shall have convinced you that he is in reality nothing but a vegetable. When I have, before your eyes, cut the throat of this vegetable, and when you see no single drop of blood follow the knife, then you will be satisfied of the truth of my assertion. Having gazed on such a specimen of Nature's jugglery, you will, I hope, do me the honor to walk up and

115

behold yet greater wonders within."

He ceased, and set about getting his knife from his pocket. Clare, watching Gunn's every motion, had partially sheltered himself behind the side of the doorway. Clare saw that his friend was in mortal peril. With the eye of one used to wild animals and the unexpectedness of their sudden motions, he stood following every movement of Gunn's hands. While Gunn held Abdiel as he did, he could not seriously injure him, although he *was* hurting him dreadfully.

When Clare saw the arm that held the dog drawn in, and the other hand move to the man's pocket, he knew that in a moment more Abdiel's body would be dashed on the ground, his head half off and the blood streaming from his neck.

Gunn had stooped a little, and slightly relaxed his hold on the dog to open his knife. With a bound that doubled the force of the blow, Clare struck Gunn on the side of the head. He had no choice where to hit him, and his fist fell on the spot recently torn by the puma's claws. The tyrant fell, and lay stunned for a moment.

Abdiel flung himself on his master. Clare picked him up and dashed down the steps, one instant before Glum Gunn rose, cursing furiously. Clare charged into the crowd: it was not a time to be civil! Abdiel's life was in imminent danger! That his own was in the same predicament did not occur to him.

Clare's sudden rush took the crowd by surprise. Some started to follow him, but the portion of the crowd he came to next closed up behind him and hid him. All the women and most of the men took the part of the boy who loved his dog.

Clare got out of the crowd, and was soon beyond sight of anyone who knew what had taken place. He hurried on, his only thought to get away from the man who would murder Abdiel.

The town was a long way behind when the question of what they were to do for supper and shelter presented itself.

This had grown a strange thought, for the caravan had been his home. Clare discovered that he was not as ready to face the hunger and cold as he had been before. At least they had more money to go on. He was glad for Abdiel that he grew his own clothes, for Clare had left his warmest behind him.

It made him ashamed to find himself regretting his clothes when he had lost a mother! Then Clare remembered that she had his sovereign, and the wages due since his clothes were paid for. The money would help to pay back Glum Gunn and set the beasts free from him. Then Clare could go back and spend his life with his mother and the puma.

It was late in the autumn. The boy and dog could do without supper, but they had to find shelter. A farmhouse came in sight. It recalled so vividly Clare's early experiences with homelessness that beasts and caravans, his mother and Glum Gunn, grew hazy and distant. Clare and Abdiel were back in the old misery—a misery in which, however, Clare's heart had not been pierced as now with pangs of innocent creatures unable or unwilling to defend themselves. It was a long time before he learned that for weeks Gunn was unable to hurt any of the animals; that his drinking, his late wound, and the blow Clare had given him had brought on him a severe infection.

When they reached the farmyard, Clare knew that the cattle and horses had been fed and put in the stables. He crept into one of the cow houses. An empty stall was before him, like a chamber prepared for his need. He gathered a few straws from under each of the cows, and spread for Abdiel and himself a thin couch. But with the excitement of what had happened, his wonder as to what would come next, and the hunger that had begun to gnaw at him, Clare could not sleep. As he lay awake, thoughts came to him.

Clare began to think how helpless he was. He was thinking of doing things for the ones he loved. But he could do nothing to deliver his mother from her villainous brother-in-law. He could do nothing more to help the puma. And Mary—he could do nothing for her.

Was it possible that he really could do nothing? Then he remembered that people used to say prayers in the days when he went with his mother to church. He had been taught to say prayers, but had begun to forget them when there was no bed to kneel beside. Did it matter that he had no church and no bedside? Surely one place must be as good as another, if it was true that God was everywhere. Surely God could hear him wherever he spoke and however low he spoke.

From the moment of that conclusion, Clare began to pray to God. And now he prayed the right kind of prayer—he asked for what he wanted. Clare only asked God to do what He was always doing. His prayer was that God would be good to all his mothers, and to his two fathers, and Mr. Halliwell, and Mary, and Susan, and his own baby, and Tommy—and to the poor puma and would, if Glum Gunn beat him, help him to bear the blows.

He ended with something like this: "God, I can't do anything for anybody! I wish I could! You can get near them, God: please do something good for every one of them—because I can't."

Having thus cast all his cares on God, Clare went to sleep and woke in the morning ready for the new day.

Over the next few weeks, Clare and Abdiel did not live on the fat of the land. But now and then some benevolent person, seeing the boy in such need, would contrive a job in order to pay him for it. In one place, although they had no need of him, certain good people gave him ten days' work with a gardener, and dismissed him with twenty shillings in his pocket.

The boy and dog were often cold and always hungry, but their lives were anything but dull. Clare wandered along, seeking work and finding next to none—all the time upheld by the feeling that something was waiting for him somewhere, that every day he was drawing nearer to it.

CHAPTER NINETEEN

Toward the Sea

Without knowing it, Clare was approaching the sea. Walking along a chain of downs, he saw it suddenly—for the first time in his memory, though not in his life. It appeared as a pale blue cloud on the horizon, between two low hills, and brought with it a strange feeling of ancient pleasure. It was the faintest revival of an all but obliterated childhood impression of something familiar, lying somewhere deeper than the memory.

The path was leading him toward one of the principal southern ports, and he perceived he was drawing near a town. He had already passed a house or two with a little lawn in front and indications of a garden behind. To door after door he carried his modest request for work: some doors were shut in his face almost before he could speak, while at others he had a civil word from maid or a rough word from man—but no work. It had become harder to find shelter.

For some days now, neither Clare nor Abdiel had come even within sight of food enough to make a meal. The dog was rather thinner than his master, but Clare had brown cheeks and clear eyes, and, save when suffering immediately from hunger, felt perfectly well.

The nights were now very cold; winter was coming fast. Had Clare been long enough in one place for people to know him, he would never have been allowed to go so cold and hungry; but he had always to move on, and nobody had time to learn to care about him.

One evening, just before sunset, grown sleepy in spite of

the gathering cold, he sat down on one of the two steep grassy slopes that bordered the road. His feet were bare, but his soles had grown like leather. Abdiel lay down on Clare's leathery feet and covered them from the night.

The sun was shooting his last radiance along the road when an elderly lady came to her gate at the top of the opposite slope, and looked along the road with the sun. Her glance fell upon the sleepers.

Her mere glance seemed to wake Abdiel, who licked at Clare's brown, dusty feet. Gently opening her gate, the woman descended the slope, crossed the road, and stood silent, regarding the outcasts.

"You shouldn't be sleeping there!" she said.

Abdiel started to his four feet and would have snarled, but one look at the lady changed his mind. Clare half awoke, half sat up, made an inarticulate murmur, and fell back again.

"Get up, my boy!" called the old lady.

"Oh, please, ma'am, must I?" answered Clare, slowly rising to his feet. "I had but just lain down, and I'm so tired! Please, ma'am, why is everybody so set against letting me sleep?"

"It's because of the frost, my boy!" she said. "It would be the death of you to sleep out of doors tonight!"

"It's a nice place for it, ma'am!"

"To sleep in? Certainly not!"

"I didn't mean that, ma'am. I meant a nice place to go away from—to die in, ma'am!"

"That is not ours to choose," answered the old lady severely, but the tone of her severity trembled.

"I won't find anywhere so nice as this bank," said Clare, turning and looking at it sorrowfully.

"There are plenty of places in town. It's but a mile farther on!"

"But this is so much nicer, ma'am! And I've no money— none at all, ma'am. When I came out of prison—"

"Came out of where?"

"Out of prison, ma'am." Clare had never been in prison in

a legal sense, never having been convicted of anything. Yet he did not know the difference between detention and imprisonment.

"How dare you mention prison!" she exclaimed, holding up her hands in horror. "And to say it so coolly too! Are you not ashamed of yourself?"

"No, ma'am."

"It's a shame to have been in prison."

"Not if I didn't do anything wrong."

"Nobody will believe that, I'm afraid!"

"I suppose not, ma'am! But the worst of it is, they won't give me any work!"

"Do you always tell people you've come out of prison?"

"Yes, ma'am, when I think of it."

"Then you can't wonder why they won't give you work!"

"There's one thing I *do* wonder at," said Clare. "When I say I've been in prison, they believe me. But when I say I haven't done anything wrong, then they mock me, and seem quite amused at being expected to believe that."

"People will always believe you against yourself. What are you going to do if nobody will give you work? You can't starve!"

"I can, ma'am! It's the one thing I've got to do. We've been pretty near the last of it sometimes—me and Abdiel. Haven't we, Abby?"

The dog wagged his tail, and the old lady turned aside to control her feelings.

"Don't cry, ma'am," Clare said. "I don't mind it—not much. I don't think it's so very bad to die of hunger!"

"If you didn't do anything wrong, what *did* you do?" asked the old lady, almost at her wits' end.

"I don't like telling things that are not going to be believed. It's like washing your face with ink!"

"I will try to believe you."

"Then I will tell you. The policeman came in the middle of the night when we were asleep, and took us all away, because we were in a house that was not ours."

"Whose was it then?"

"Nobody knew. It was what they call in chancery. There was nobody in it but moths and flies and spiders and rats—though I think the rats only came to eat the baby."

"Baby! Then your whole family—father, mother, and all—were taken to prison!"

"No, ma'am—my fathers and my mothers were taken up into the dome of the angels. I have two fathers and two mothers up there, and one mother in this world. She's the mother of the wild beasts."

The old lady began to doubt Clare's sanity, but went on questioning him. "How did you have a baby with you?"

"The baby was my own, ma'am. I took her out of the water barrel."

Once more Clare had to tell his story—from the time, that is, when his adoptive father and mother died. He told it in such a simple matter-of-fact way, yet with such quaint remarks that if the old lady was not quite able to believe his tale, it was because she thought the boy was one of God's innocents, with an angel-haunted brain.

"And what's become of Tommy?" she asked.

"He's in the same workhouse with the baby. I'm very glad, for I had nothing to give him to eat. He would have been sure to steal. I couldn't have kept him from it!"

"You must be more careful of your company."

"Please, ma'am, I was very careful of Tommy. He had the best company I could give him. I did try to be better for Tommy's sake. But my trying wasn't much use to Tommy, so long as he wouldn't try! If I had him now, and could give him plenty to eat, and had the baby as well as Abdiel to help me, we might make something of Tommy, I think. Don't you, Abdiel?"

The dog, who had stood looking in his master's face all the time he spoke, wagged his tail faster.

"What a name to give a dog? Where did you find it?"

"In *Paradise Lost*, ma'am. Abdiel was the one angel, you remember, ma'am, who, when he saw what Satan was up to,

left him and went back to do what God told him. I love
Abdiel, and because I loved the little dog and he took care of
the baby, I called him Abdiel too."

"But how dare you give the name of an angel to a dog!"

"To a good dog, ma'am! A good dog is good enough to go
with any angel—at his heels of course! Abdiel won't mind—
the angel Abdiel, I mean, ma'am—he won't mind lending his
name to my friend. The dog will have a name of his own,
perhaps, someday—like the rest of us!"

"What is your name?"

"The name I have now is like the dog's—a borrowed one."

Clare had grown very white. He sat down, and lay back on
the grass. He had talked more in those minutes than he had
for weeks, and hunger had made him weak.

"What a wicked old woman I am!" said the lady to herself.
She ran across the road like a little long-legged bird and
climbed the bank swiftly. She disappeared, but soon returned with a tumbler of milk and a huge piece of bread.

"Here, boy!" she cried. "Hurry and eat this."

Clare sat up feebly, and stared at the tumbler for a moment. When he had it in his hand, he held it out to the dog.

"Here, Abdiel, have a little," he said.

This offended the old lady. "You're *never* going to give the
dog that good milk!" she cried.

"A little of it, please, ma'am!"

"And feed him out of the tumbler too?"

"He's had nothing today, ma'am, and we're comrades!"

"But it's not clean of you!"

"Ah, you don't know dogs, ma'am! His tongue is as clean
as anybody's."

Abdiel took three or four little laps of the milk, drew away,
and looked up at his master—as if to say, "You, now!"

"Besides," Clare went on, "he couldn't get at it so well in
the bottom of the tumbler."

With that he raised it to his own lips, drank eagerly, and
set it on the road half empty, smiling his thanks to the giver.
Then he broke the bread, and gave the dog nearly half of it.

He ate the rest himself. The old lady stood looking on in silence, wondering what to do with this celestial beggar.

"Would you mind sleeping in the greenhouse, if I had a bed put up for you?" she asked.

"I would rather stay here," said Clare.

"Why?"

"Because you don't quite believe me, ma'am. You wouldn't be able to sleep for thinking that a boy just out of prison was lying in your greenhouse. No, ma'am, thank you! After such a supper, Abdiel and I shall sleep beautifully! Perhaps, you could give me a job in your garden tomorrow."

The old lady took the tumbler from the boy's hand and went into the house. But in two minutes she came out again with another great piece of bread for Clare, and a bone with something on it which she threw to Abdiel. The dog's ears started up and his eyes gleamed; but he would not touch the bone without Clare's approval. Once given, the dog fell upon it, and worried it as if it had been a rat.

When the old lady left them for the third time, Clare walked with her across the way, bread in his hand, to open the gate for her. When she was inside, he took off his cap and bade her goodnight with a grace that won her heart.

Before she had taken three steps from the gate, she turned. "Boy!" she called, "I shall not be able to sleep for thinking of you out there in the bleak night!"

"I am used to it, ma'am!"

"But you see I'm not! You may like hoarfrost sheets, but I don't! What if you should die from the frost? I should never go to bed again with a good conscience!"

"I will do whatever you please, ma'am," he answered humbly. "Come, Abdiel!"

In half an hour, Clare and his four-footed angel were asleep in a comfortable bed in an outbuilding.

CHAPTER TWENTY
A Safe Harbor

Since his hostess gave him no answer when he asked about a job in her garden, Clare concluded that she would be relieved if he left. When he woke in the morning, therefore, he walked out of the gate, crossed the road, and sat down on the spot he had occupied the night before, although he could not linger within gates where he was unknown, neither could he slink away without morning thanks for the gift of a warm night. As he sat, he grew drowsy and fell fast asleep.

The thoughts of his hostess had been running on very different lines. She wanted to do something to help the boy, but as for giving him work, her problem was the gardener, John. She rose earlier than usual, and went down to the gate to meet John so they could talk the thing over.

"Good gracious!" she murmured aloud, "does it rain beggars?" For there, on the same spot, lay what she thought was another beggar, with a dog exactly like the one from the day before. She did not feel moved to make his acquaintance.

As she mounted the steps, she caught sight of the gardener at the other gate, casting a displeased look across the road at the tramp.

The gardener came in, and his mistress joined him and walked with him to his work. She told him as much as she thought fit concerning the boy, and hinted of their duty to give everyone a chance. At last John consented to let the boy help him for a day.

She had just won the gardener's consent when the cook came running to say the boy was gone. The old lady stood for a moment with her eyes on the ground. Then she ran to the gate and straight down the bank to the road. The cook, who had followed, saw her mistress standing over a boy asleep on the grass of the opposite bank.

Abdiel, lying on Clare's bosom, watched her with keen friendly eyes.

"No!" said Miss Tempest to herself. "There's no duplicity there!"

Clare opened his eyes, and started lightly to his feet. "Good morning, ma'am!" he said, pulling off his cap.

"Good morning. What am I to call you?" she asked.

"Clare, if you please, ma'am."

"Well, Clare, I've been talking to my gardener about you," said Miss Tempest. "He will give you a job."

"God bless you, ma'am! I'm ready!" cried Clare, stretching out his arms, as if to get them to the proper length for work. "Where shall I find him?"

"You must have breakfast first." She led the way to the kitchen, where the cook looked at the dog, her face puckered all over.

"Please, cook, will you give this young man some breakfast? He wanted to go to work without any, but that wouldn't do," said her mistress.

"I hope the dog won't be running in and out of my kitchen all day, ma'am!"

"No fear of that, cook!" said Clare. "He never leaves me."

"Then I don't think—I'm afraid that John," she began, and stopped. "But that's none of my business," she added.

Miss Tempest said nothing, but trembled a little. John, the gardener, had a perfect hatred of dogs.

The cook threw the dog a crust of bread, and Abdiel, after a look at his master, fell upon it with his white, hungry little teeth. Then she made a cup of coffee for Clare, casting an occasional glance of pity at his worn clothes and his brown bare feet.

"How do you expect to work in the garden without shoes?" she asked.

"Most things I can do well enough without them," answered Clare. "Even digging, if the ground is not very hard. My feet used to be soft, but now the soles of them are like leather. They've grown their own shoes," he added, with a smile, and looked straight in her eyes.

The smile and the look went far to win her heart, and she wondered how such a fair-spoken, sweet-faced boy could be a tramp. She poured him a huge cup of coffee, fried him a piece of bacon, and cut him as much bread and butter as he could eat. The cook fed the dog with equal liberality. Then, curious to witness their reception by John, with whom she had a continuous feud, she took Clare to the gardener.

From a distance, John saw them coming. With an irate look fixed upon the dog, he started to meet them. Clare knew too well the meaning of that look.

The moment he came near enough, without a word John raised his sharp hoe and made a sudden downstroke toward the dog. But Abdiel darted aside; the weapon came down on the hard gravel, jarring the man's arm.

Cursing, John followed him and made another attempt, which Abdiel in like manner eluded. John followed and followed; Abdiel fled and fled—never farther than a few yards, always dodging the blows which the gardener aimed at him. Fruitlessly Clare assured him that the dog would do him no harm. At last John desisted, wiped his forehead with his shirt-sleeve, and turned upon Clare in the smothered wrath that knows itself ridiculous.

"Awa', ye deil's buckie," he cried, "an' tak' the little Sawtan wi'ye! Dinna let me see yer face again."

"But the lady told me you would give me a job!" said Clare.

"I didna tell her I wad gie yer tyke a job! I wad though, gien he wad lat me!"

"He's given you a stiff one!" said the cook, and laughed again.

The gardener took no notice of her remark. "Awa' wi' ye!" he cried again, yet more wrathfully. "Or—"

He raised his hand.

Clare looked in his eyes and did not budge.

"For shame, John!" scolded the cook. "Would you strike a child?"

"I'm no child," Clare said. "He can't hurt me much. I've had a good breakfast!"

"Lat 'im tak' awa' that deevil o' a tyke o' his, as I told him," thundered the gardener, "or I'll mak' a pulp o' 'im!"

"I've had such a breakfast, sir, as I'm bound to give a whole day's work in return for," said Clare, looking up at the angry man, "and I won't stir till I've done it. Stolen food on my stomach would make me sick!"

"Ye'll hae to tak' some ither mode o' paying' the debt!" said John. "Stick spade in yird here, ye sall not! Ye or I maun flit first!" He walked slowly away, shouldering his hoe.

"Come, Abdiel," said Clare. "We must go and tell Miss Tempest! Perhaps she'll find something else for us to do."

The gardener half turned, as if he would speak, but changed his mind and went his way.

"Never mind John!" said the cook, loud enough for John to hear. "He's an old curmudgeon who can't sleep o' nights for quarrelin' inside him. I'll go to mis'ess, and you go and sit down in the kitchen till I come to you."

Clare went into the kitchen and sat down. The housemaid came in, and asked him what he wanted there.

"Cook told me to wait here till she came to me," he answered. "She's gone to speak to Miss Tempest."

"I won't have that dog here."

"When I had a home," remarked Clare, "our servant said the cook was queen of the kitchen. I don't want to be rude, ma'am, but I must do as she told me."

"She never told you to bring that mangy animal in here!"

"She knew he would follow me, and she said nothing about him. But he's not mangy. He hasn't enough to eat to be mangy. He's as lean as a dried fish!"

"You won't let him put his nose in anything, will you?" she asked.

"Abdiel is much too much of a gentleman to do it," he answered.

Miss Tempest and Mrs. Mereweather had all this time been talking about what was to be done with the boy. They agreed it was too bad that anyone willing to work should be stopped by the bad temper of a gardener. The cook had taken such a fancy to Clare that she wanted him to work in the house as a page. Miss Tempest greatly desired the same thing and was delighted when Mrs. Mereweather suggested it. The only obstacle was the dog. "It's all right, Clare," said Mrs. Mereweather, returning to the kitchen. "You're to help me in the kitchen—an' if you can do what you're told an' are willin' to learn, we'll soon get you out of your troubles. There's but one thing in the way."

"What is it?" asked Clare.

"The dog, of course! You must part with the dog."

"That I cannot do," returned Clare quietly, but with countenance fallen and sorrowful. "Come, Abdiel!"

"You don't mean you're going to walk off in such an ungrateful fashion—an' all for a miserable dog!" exclaimed the cook.

"The lady has been most kind to us, and we're grateful to her, and ready to work for her if she will let us—ain't we, Abdiel? But Abdiel has done far more for me than Miss Tempest! To part with Abdiel, and leave him to starve, or get into bad company, would be sheer ingratitude. Besides, he wouldn't leave me. He would be always hanging about."

"But you don't really mean that you'd go off again on the tramp, to be as cold and hungry again tomorrow as you were yesterday—and all for the sake of a dog? A dog ain't a Christian!"

"Abdiel's more of a Christian than some I know," answered Clare. "He does what his master tells him."

"There's something in that!" said the cook.

"If I parted with Abdiel, I could never hold up my head among the angels," insisted Clare. "Think what harm it might do him! He could trust nobody after that; his goodness might give way! I've got to take care of Abdiel, and Abdiel's got to take care of me—ain't you, Abby?"

"We can't have him here in the kitchen!" said the cook in relenting tone.

"I know what I shall do!" cried Clare, in sudden resolve. "I will ask Miss Tempest to keep him upstairs with her, and when she is tired of either of us, we will go away together."

"Miss Tempest would be eaten alive with fleas in ten minutes!"

"No fear of that!" rejoined Clare. "Abdiel catches all his own fleas! Let me have a tub of warm water and a bit of soap, and I'll show you a body of hair to astonish you."

"What breed is he?" asked the housemaid.

"Mostly the sky-blue terrier sort."

They got Clare a tub and plenty of warm water, and he washed Abdiel thoroughly. Taken out and dried, he seemed no more unfit for a lady's chamber.

"Will you please ask Miss Tempest if I may bring him on to the lawn, and show her some of his tricks?" Clare said.

The good lady was pleased with the cleverness and instant obedience of the little animal. Clare proposed that she should keep him by her.

"But will he stay with me? And will he do what I tell him?" she asked.

Clare took the dog aside, and talked to him. He told him what he was going to do, and what he expected of him. When his master laid him down at Miss Tempest's feet, there he lay—and when Clare went with the cook, the dog did not move, though he cast many wistful glances after the lord of his heart. When his new mistress went into the house, he followed her submissively, his head hanging and his tail motionless. He soon seemed to know that his friend had not abandoned him.

CHAPTER TWENTY-ONE

A Surprise in the Night

Mrs. Mereweather took much pleasure in going to town in the omnibus* to buy clothing for Clare. In a few days she had him dressed in a plain suit of dark blue cloth. Thus dressed, he looked as much of a gentleman as before: his look of refinement had owed nothing to the contrast of his rags.

As the days went on, Mrs. Mereweather was not once disappointed in Clare. He did everything with such a will that both she and the housemaid were always ready to stop and help him. And nothing could be kinder than the way his mistress treated him. She lent him some books, perceived that he not only read but respected them, and so let him have the run of her library when his day's work was over.

Clare made good use of his privileges. He read whatever came in his way, and learned more than most boys at school, more even than most young men at college—for it is not what one knows, but what one uses, that is the true measure of learning.

People wondered how Miss Tempest had managed to find such a nice-looking page,* and the good lady was flattered by their wonder. But she knew the world too well to be sure of him yet.

Miss Tempest was the last of an old family, with no living relatives in the world. Hence the pieces of personal property that had been passed down through the family had mostly drifted into Miss Tempest's life. She did not think often of their value: had she done so, she would have kept them at her banker's. But she valued them greatly both for their beauty and their associations, constantly using as many of them as she could.

Many of her friends had tried to persuade her that it was not wise to have so many valuables in the house. At times she would think about sending her valuables to the bank; but she always said, "Of what use will they be at the bank? I might as well not have them at all! Better sell them and do some good with the money! No, I must have them about me!"

It was well now for Miss Tempest that she was so faithful herself as to encourage faithfulness in others: gladly would she have had Abdiel sleep in her room, but she would not take the pleasure of his nightly company from Clare. The dog therefore slept on the boy's bed.

One night, about half-past twelve, Abdiel sprang up at his master's feet, listened a moment, and gave a low growl. Clare woke, and found his bed trembling with the tremor of his little four-footed guardian. Telling him to keep quiet, Clare rose on his elbow, and listened, but could hear nothing. He thought then he would light his candle and go down, but decided to go down without a light and listen in darkness. He crept out of bed, and went first to the small open window in the narrow gable-wall of his attic room. He thought he heard a light movement below. Very softly he put out his head and looked down. There was no moon, but in the momentary flash of a lantern he saw a small pair of legs disappearing inside the scullery* window, which was almost under his own. Swift and noiseless Clare hurried down, and reached the scullery door just in time for a little fellow who came stealing out of it, to run against him.

Clare realized that the legs were those of a boy sent in to open a door or window. When the boy, feeling his way in the dark, came against him, Clare gripped him by the throat with the squeeze that used to silence Tommy. The prowler knew the squeeze, and surprised Clare by whispering, "Clare! Clare! They said they'd kill me if I didn't open the door for them."

"If you utter one whimper, I'll throttle you," said Clare. He tightened his grasp for an instant, and Tommy, who had not forgotten that Clare did what he said, immediately gave in, and was led away. Clare took Tommy in his arms and carried him to his room, tied him hand and foot, and left him on the floor, fastened to the bedstead. Then Clare crept swiftly to the servants' room, wakened them, told them what he had done, and asked them to help him.

Both women undertook at once to do their part. But when he proposed that they should open a window, as if it were done by Tommy, and entice the burglars to enter, they, naturally declined.

The burglars outside were perplexed by the lack of any sign from Tommy. Then it occurred to Clare that he had left the scullery window unwatched. He and the two women servants hurried to it and were just in time: two long thin legs were sticking through.

Clare saw that as long as that body filled the window, no other body would pass that way, and it would be well to keep it there—like a cork to the house. He begged the women to lay hold each of an ankle, and stick to it like a clamp, while he ran to get some string.

The women clutched and held on bravely. The owner of the legs made vigorous efforts to release them, more anxious a good deal to get out than he had been to get in, but he was not very strong, and had no leverage. The women laid hold of him and pulled away from each other, and so made of his legs a wedge.

Clare came back with pieces of clothesline, which he slipped with a running knot around both ankles. Then he drew the lines over two hooks in the ceiling, some distance apart, hauled the feet up as high as he could, and fastened the ends of the lines. It was now impossible to pull the fellow out.

Leaving the women to watch, Clare went to his room and looked from the window. Right under him stood a short, burly figure, while another man was taking intermittent hauls at the arms of their leg-tied companion, regardless of his stifled cries of pain. Clare went and got his half-full waterjug, leaned out once more, and dropped it. The jug fell and knocked the breath out of the burly man. He lay motionless, and the other man fled.

The window-stopper, hearing the crash of the jug, wrenched and kicked and struggled, but in vain. Then he pretended to be all but dead, thinking to move their pity and be set free. But Clare went to the next house and got one of the servants there to go for the police, begging him to hurry—for Clare knew that if Miss Tempest came down before the police arrived, she would certainly let the fellow in the window go, and Tommy with him. But Clare was determined the law should have its way.

The stout man was gone. He had risen and staggered into the shrubbery, and there fallen, but had risen once more and got away.

Going at last to his room, Clare proceeded to wash and dress. Tommy lay staring, his old contempt for Clare revived. "I want to go," he said. "I ain't done nothing."

"Go, then," said Clare, and took no more heed of him.

Tommy, who was still tied to the bed, changed his tone. "Please, Clare, let me go," he whined.

"I will not. You must go with the police."

The police came. When they untied and drew out the "cork" from the scullery window, Clare thought he had seen him before, but could not remember where. One of the policemen, however, cried out joyfully, "Aha, my boy! I've been a looking' for you!"

"Never set eyes on ye afore," growled the fellow.

"Don't ye say now ye ain't a dear friend o' mine," insisted the policeman, "when I carry yer pictur' in my bosom!"

He pulled out his pocketbook and took from it a photograph, and compared it with the face before him. Clare recognized the boy as the same one sent by Maidstone to exchange bandboxes with him.

"Her majesty the Queen wants you for that robbery, you

know!" said the policeman.

Profiting, doubtless, by Maidstone's own example, the fellow had, as Clare now learned, run away from his master, carrying with him the contents of the till.

The leader of the gang, injured by Clare's waterjug, was soon after captured, and the gang was broken up.

When Miss Tempest's friends first heard of the attempted break-in, they wondered what she could expect if she took tramps into her service! They were considerably astonished, however, when they read in the newspaper how the magistrate had spoken of the admirable courage of Miss Tempest's page, and the resolution with which the women of her household had helped him.

After the trial, Clare begged and was granted an interview with the magistrate. He told him what he knew about Tommy, and asked that Tommy might be sent to some reformatory, to be kept from bad company until he was able to distinguish between right and wrong. The magistrate promised it would be done, and with kind words dismissed him.

Things returned to their old way at Miss Tempest's. Her friends never doubted she would send her valuables to her banker's strong room, but they found themselves mistaken. She was convinced that, with such servants and Abdiel, her belongings were safe where they were.

CHAPTER TWENTY-TWO
The Bank

Even after two years Clare never came to regard Miss Tempest as his fourth mother. She was truly good and kind, but she had a certain manner which prevented him from feeling entirely comfortable with her. He knew that Abdiel was thoroughly at ease in her company, and he believed that the dog knew her better than he did.

It was natural that, after the defeated robbery, Clare should become better known to Miss Tempest's friends. Therefore, Miss Tempest spoke to her banker concerning Clare's ability, mentioning that in his spare time, he had been reading hard, as well as attending an evening school for mathematics, where he gained his teacher's approval.

The banker listened solemnly. No one ever could tell what Mr. Shotover was thinking: his face was more a mask than a face. High in the world's regard, rich, and of unquestioned integrity, he kept his affairs to himself. He was a constant churchgoer and giver of money. Priding himself on his moral discrimination, he had, now and then, taken a young man from a lower position and put him to work in the bank.

He had had his eye on Clare ever since reading the newspaper story about the robbery and the magistrate's words of praise for the boy. But something in the boy repelled him. Moved, however, by Miss Tempest's opinion and by a desire to discover that the boy was a hypocrite, Mr. Shotover consented to give him a trial. Miss Tempest hurried to tell Clare the grand thing she had done for him.

She was disappointed at the coolness and lack of interest with which Clare heard her great news. She was glad that he did not want to leave her, but she was annoyed that he seemed unaware of any advantage to be gained in doing so.

Clare agreed to go to work at the bank, even though he had to leave Abdiel in Miss Tempest's care. At the bank Clare had to take the lowest and most menial position. He was required to be at work a half hour earlier than the others, to be the last to go away at night, and to sleep in the Shotovers' house—where a room in the attic was given to him.

Mr. Shotover himself lived above the bank with his wife and two daughters. Mrs. Shotover suffered from a terrible disease—that of thinking herself ill when nothing was the matter with her. The elder daughter was a high-spirited girl about twenty, with a frank, friendly manner. The younger girl was about six, of whom the mother took not so much care by half as a tigress of her cub.

One morning as Clare was coming down from his room to open the windows of the bank, he almost tumbled over a child on the dim twisting attic stair. The little girl gave a low cry and started to run away. But the moment she saw Clare's smile, she knew the soul that was the light of the smile. Her doll dropped from her hands as she raised them to lay her arms gently around Clare's neck.

"Oh!" she said. "You've come!"

He saw a pale, ordinary little face, with large gray eyes, a tiny, upturned nose, and a pretty mouth.

"Yes, little one. Were you expecting me?" he returned, with his arms about her.

"Yes," she answered, in the tone of one stating what the other must know.

"How was it I frightened you, then?"

"Only at first. I thought you was an ogre! That was before I saw you. Then I knew!"

"Who told you I was coming?"

"Nobody. Nobody knew you was coming but me. I've known it ever since I was born—I think!" She turned her head a little and looked down where the doll lay a step or two below.

"You can go now, dolly," she said. "I don't want you any more." Here she paused a while, as if listening to a reply, then went on, "I am much obliged to you, dolly—but what am I to do with you? I did my best to get you to be somebody, but you wouldn't! I will take you and put you where you can be as dull as you please, and nobody will mind." Here she left Clare, went down, and lifted her plaything. "Dolly, dolly," she resumed, "he's come! I knew he would!"

Without looking back, she went slowly down the steps with the doll in her arms.

Clare saw nothing more of her that day, but his work seemed to be not half as dull as it had been before. To know that a child who already loved him was in the house changed the stupid bank almost into the dome of the angels.

As Clare came down the next morning, there was the child again on the dark, narrow stair. She had no doll. Her hands lay folded in her lap.

"Where's dolly?" asked Clare.

"Buried. I threw her out of the window."

"Into the street?"

"Yes. She fell on a horse's back, and he jumped. I was sorry."

"It didn't hurt him. I hope it didn't hurt dolly!"

She answered, "Things don't be hurt! Dolly was a thing! She's no thing now!"

"Will you tell me, please," he said, "when a thing is only a thing?"

"When it won't mind what you do or say to it."

"And when is a thing no thing any more?"

"When you never think of it again."

Clare thought that was enough metaphysics for one morning. "I waited for you yesterday," he said, "but you didn't come!"

"Dolly didn't like to be buried. I mean, I didn't like burying dolly. I cried and wouldn't come."

"I see! But what have you to play with now?"

"I don't want to play now. You've come! I'm growed up!"

"Yes, of course!" answered Clare. But he was puzzled what to say next.

What could he do for her? He would gladly have spent the day with her but there was his work which had to be done.

"I wish I could stay with you all day!" he said. "But your papa wants me in the bank. I must go." He paused, then said, "Is there anything I can do for you before I go—for I must go?"

"Who says *must* to you? The nurse says *must* to me."

"Your papa says *must* to me."

"If you didn't say *yes* when Papa said *must*, what would come next?"

"He would say, 'Go out of my house, and never come in again.' "

"If I didn't say *yes* when Papa said *must*, what would happen?"

"He would try to make you say it."

"And if I wouldn't, would he say, 'Go out of my house and never come in again'?"

"No, you are his little girl!"

"Then I think he shouldn't say it to you. What is your name?"

"Clare."

"Then, Clare, if my papa sends you out of his house, I will go with you. You wouldn't turn me out, would you, when I was a little naughty?"

"If he turned you out, it would be all the same. Where you go, I will go. I must you know! Would you mind if he said, 'Go away'?"

"I should be very sorry to leave you."

"Yes, but that's not going to be! Why do you stay with Papa? Were you in the house long before I saw you?"

"No, only a very little while."

"Did you come in from the street?"

"Yes, I came in from the street. Your papa pays me to work for him."

"And if you wouldn't?"

"Then I should have no money, and nothing to eat, and nowhere to sleep at night."

"Would that make you 'uncomfable'? "

"It would make me die."

"Have you a papa?"

"Yes, but he's far away."

"You could go to him, couldn't you?"

"One day I shall."

"Why don't you go now, and take me?"

"Because he died—went away out of sight, where we can't go to look for him till we go out of sight too."

"When will that be?"

"I don't know, and nobody knows."

"Then perhaps you will never go?"

"We must go—it's only that nobody knows when."

"I think the when that nobody knows may not ever come. And why didn't you come ever so much sooner? Why did you make me wait for you all the time?"

"Nobody ever told me you were waiting."

"Nobody ever told me you were coming, but I knew."

"You had to wait for me, and you knew. I had to wait for you, and I didn't know! When we have time, I will tell you all about myself, and how I've been waiting too."

"Waiting for me?"

"No. For my father and mother—and for somebody else, I think."

"That's me."

"No, I'm waiting yet. I didn't know I was coming to you till I came, and there you were!"

The child was silent for a moment. Then she said thoughtfully, "You will tell me all about yourself! That will be nice! Can you tell me stories?"

"I can sometimes. But now I must go, or I shall be late, and nobody ever ought to be late."

"Go then. I will go to my room and wait again." She went down the stairs without once looking behind her.

All day Clare kept thinking about what could he do for the little girl. Perhaps what stirred his feeling for her most was a suspicion that she was neglected. He could tell by the solemnly still ways of the child, that she was often left to her own resources.

After much thinking, he concluded that he must wait: opportunity might suggest something—and he would rather find than make an opportunity!

He had not long to wait. That very afternoon, taking a message for the head clerk, he saw Ann walking with her older sister. Ann was very white, and so tired that she could but drag her little feet after her. Miss Shotover, flushed with exertion, held Ann tight and hauled her along by the hand. Every now and then she would give the little arm a pull and say, though not very crossly, "Do come along!"

Coming nearer, Clare stopped and lifted his hat, and then the dazed child saw him. She said not a word, uttered no sound, only drew her hand from her sister's, and held up her arms to Clare. He picked her up.

"I beg your pardon, Miss Shotover," he said, "but the little one and I have met before. If you will allow me, I will carry her. She looks tired!"

Miss Shotover was glad to be relieved of her sister, and gave smiling consent. "If you would be so kind as to carry her home," she said, "I would be able to do a little shopping!"

"You will not mind my taking her a little farther first, ma'am? I am delivering a message for Mr. Woolrige. I will carry her all the way, and be very careful of her."

Miss Shotover was not one to cherish anxiety. She already knew Clare, and willingly yielded. Saying, with one of her pleasant smiles, that she would hold him accountable for her, she sailed away, like a sloop that had been dragging her anchor but had now cut her cable. Clare thought what a sweet-looking girl she was—and in truth she was sweet-

looking. Then his heart turned to the little one in his arms.

What a walk that was for both of them! Little Ann seemed never to have lived before: she was actually happy! She had long been waiting for Clare, and he had come! To be in Clare's arms was better than being in the little house on the elephant's back in her best picture book!

And to Clare, what a glory it was to have a human child in his arms! He was not going to forget Abdiel. Abdiel was not a fact to be forgotten—he was a true heart, a live soul, and Clare would love him forever—not an atom less now that he had one upon whom a larger love was able to flow!

To the pale-faced, listening child, Clare talked much about the wonderful Abdiel, and about the good Miss Tempest who was keeping the dog to live again one day with his old master. Ann loved the dog she had never seen because the dog loved Clare.

When they returned, Clare rang the doorbell, and gave Ann to the man who opened the door. The child submitted to be taken from Clare's loving embrace, and carried to a nurse who was neither glad nor sorry to see her.

Clare had been gone so long that Mr. Woolrige found fault with him for it. Clare told him he had met Miss Shotover with her sister, and the child seemed so tired he had asked to carry her home. Mr. Woolrige was not pleased, but he said nothing. From that moment on, the clerks nicknamed Clare "Nursie," and Clare did his best to justify the name. He always answered when they summoned him by it.

Before the week was ended, he met with Miss Shotover, and asked her whether he could take little Ann out for a walk whenever the evening was fine. For at five o'clock the doors of the bank were shut, and half an hour afterward he was free. Miss Shotover said she saw no objection, and would tell the nurse to have Ann ready as often as the weather was fit.

The summer came and was peculiarly fine, and almost every evening Clare could be seen taking Ann for a walk. He always had little Ann in his arms, or led her along with care and attention.

The pair came speedily to understand and communicate like brother and sister. When they walked hand in hand, Clare told her stories of his life and adventures. When he carried her, he told her fairy tales, which he could spin like a spider.

So neither the bank nor the nursery was dreary any longer.

At length came the gray, brooding winter. But it was not unfriendly to little Ann. True, she was not permitted to go out in the evening anymore, but Clare, with the help of the cook, spent his dinner-hour with her instead.

CHAPTER TWENTY-THREE

A Council of Hate

The head clerk, Mr. Woolrige, thought Clare would never make a man of business: the boy did not seem to have his heart in it. But if, to be a man of business, it is not enough to do one's duty scrupulously, but the very heart must be in it, then there is something wrong with business. Mr. Woolrige passed no such judgment, however, upon certain older young men in the bank whose hearts certainly were not in the business, but in even worse places.

Clare had been in the bank more than a year, and not yet had Mr. Shotover discovered why he did not quite trust him. Had Clare known he did not, he would have wondered that he trusted him with Ann.

One evening in the early summer, when Clare and Ann had resumed their walks after five o'clock, they saw, in a waste place where houses had been going to be built for the last two years, a number of caravans drawn up in order. A rush of hope filled Clare's heart. What if it should be the menagerie he knew so well? Sure enough, there was Mr. Halliwell superintending operations! But if Glum Gunn were about, he might find it awkward with the child in his arms! Gunn might not respect even her! Besides, he ought to ask leave to take Ann to see his third mother and all his old friends, the puma and the lion and the rest of the creatures.

Little Ann was eager to know what those curious houses on wheels were. Clare told her they were like Noah's ark— full of real, live beasts. She wanted to see them. But Clare told her he could not take her without first asking permission from her parents.

"You see, little one," he explained, "you were theirs before I came! You were sent to them. You are their own little girl, and we must mind what they would like!"

"It was only till you came!" she argued. "They don't care very much for me. Ask them, please, to sell me to you. I don't think they would want much money for me! How many shillings do you think I am worth, Clare?"

"You are worth more than all the money in your papa's bank," answered Clare, looking down at her lovingly.

The child's face fell. "Am I?" she said. "I'm so sorry! I didn't know I was worth so much!" she added, with a sigh that seemed to come from the very heart of her being. "Then you're not able to buy me?"

"No, indeed, little one," answered Clare. "Besides, papas don't sell their little girls!"

"Oh, yes, they do! Gus said so to Trudie!"

Clare knew that Trudie meant her sister Gertrude.

"Who is Gus?" he asked.

"Trudie calls him Gus. I don't know more name to him. Perhaps they call him something else in the bank."

"Oh! He's in the bank, is he?" returned Clare. "Then I think I know him."

"He said it to her one night in my room. Nurse went down, and I was in my bed. They talked such a long time! I tried to go to sleep, but I couldn't. I heard all what he said to her. It wasn't half so nice as what you talk to me!"

This was not pleasant news to Clare. Augustus Marway was, if half the tales of him were true, no fit person for Gertrude to be seeing. Clare had once heard Mr. Shotover speak about gambling in most severe terms—yet it was well known in the bank that Marway spent his time with gamblers almost every night.

Clare felt sure Mr. Shotover either did not know that Marway gambled, or did not know that he talked to Gertrude. But Clare could do nothing without telling, and they all said none but the lowest of cads would carry tales! For the young men thought it right to stick by each other, and hide from Mr. Shotover some things he had a right to know. But Clare saw that no matter what they might think, he must take action.

Little Ann wondered why Clare scarcely spoke to her all the way home. But she did not say anything, for she too was troubled: she did not belong to Clare so much as she had thought she did!

Clare carried Ann to the nursery, then set out for the menagerie. When he knocked at the door of the house caravan, Mrs. Halliwell opened it, stared hardly an instant, threw her arms around his neck, and kissed him.

"Come in, come in, my boy!" she said. "It makes me a happy woman to see you again. I've been just miserable over what might have happened to you, and me with all that money of yours! I've got it by me safe, ready for you! I lie awake nights and fancy Gunn has got hold of you, and made away with you—then I fall asleep and am sure of it. He's been gone several times, looking for you, I know! I think he's afraid of you; I know he hates you. Mind you keep out of his sight—he'll give you trouble if he has the chance. He's the same as ever, a man to make life miserable."

"I've never done him wrong," said Clare, "and I'm not going to keep out of his way as if I were afraid of him! I mean to come and see the animals tomorrow."

They talked a great deal as they had their tea together. Mr. Halliwell, who did not care for tea, came and went several times, and now the night was dark. Then they spoke again of Gunn.

"Well, I don't think he'll venture to interfere with you," said Mrs. Halliwell, "unless he happens to be drunk. But who's that talking? Listen."

For some time Clare had been conscious of the whispered sounds of a dialogue somewhere near, but had paid no attention. The voices were now plainer than at first. One voice was that of old Mr. Lewin, whom he had seen several times at the bank. As the talking went on, Clare recognized the other voice also: Augustus Marway. The two fancied themselves against a caravan full of wild beasts.

Marway was the son of the port admiral who, late in life, married a silly woman. She died young, but not before she had ruined her son, whose choice company was the least respectable of the officers who came ashore from the king's ships. Recently Marway had been gambling more and having worse luck, and had borrowed until no one would lend him money. His father knew, in a vague way, how he was going on, and had nearly lost hope of his reformation. Mr. Shotover was a connection by marriage, which gave Marway the privilege of being regarded by Gertrude Shotover as a cousin—a privilege with desirable possibilities, making him anxious to retain the good opinion of his employer.

Clare heard but a portion of the conversation going on outside the wooden wall. But it was plain that Marway was pressing a creditor to leave him alone until he was married, when he would pay every shilling he owed him.

Clare heard the moneylender grant Marway a renewal for three months when, if Marway did not pay, or were not the accepted suitor of the lady whose fortune was to redeem him, his creditor would take his course.

The moment he perceived they were about to leave, Clare left the caravan and went along the edge of the waste ground, so as to meet Marway on his road back to the town. At the corner of the road they bumped together.

"Well?" he asked.

"Mr. Marway," began Clare, "I heard a great deal of your talk with old Lewin."

"A sneaking spy!"

"Nobody minds being overheard who hasn't something to hide! If I had low secrets, I would not stand up against the side of a caravan when I wanted to talk about them. I was inside. Not to hear you I would have had to stop up my ears."

"Why didn't you, then, you lowbred flunky?"

"Because I had heard of you what made it my duty to listen."

Marway cursed his arrogance, and asked what he was doing in such a place. He would report Clare, he said.

"What I was doing is *my* business," answered Clare. "Had I known you for an honest man, I would not have listened to yours. I should have had no right."

"You tell me to my face I'm a swindler!" said Marway between his teeth, letting out a blow at Clare, which he cleverly dodged.

"I do!"

"I don't know what you mean, but bitterly you shall repent, you prying rascal! To dog me and get hold of my affairs! You're going to turn informer next, of course, and bear false witness against your neighbor! You shall repent it, I swear!"

"Will it be bearing false witness to say that Miss Shotover does not know the sort of man who wants to marry her? Does she know why you want to marry her? Does her father know that you are in the clutches of a moneylender?"

Marway caught hold of Clare and threatened to kill him. Clare did not flinch, and he calmed down a little. "What do you want to square it?" he growled.

"I don't understand you," returned Clare.

"What bribe will silence you?"

"If I had meant to hold my tongue, I should have held it."

"What do you want then?"

"To keep you from marrying Miss Shotover."

"And suppose I kick you into the gutter, and tell you to mind your own business—what then?"

"I will tell either your father or Mr. Shotover all about it."

"Even *you* can't be such a fool! What good would it do you? You're not after her yourself, are you? Ha! But come, where's the use? Here—I'll give you twenty pounds, you idiot!"

"Mr. Marway, nothing will make me hold my tongue—not even your promise to drop the thing."

"Then what made you come and tell me?"

"I came to you for my own sake, because I will do nothing underhanded!"

"What are you going to do next, then?"

"I am going to tell Mrs. Shotover or Admiral Marway—I haven't yet made up my mind which."

"What are you going to tell them?"

"That old Lewin has given you three months to get engaged to Miss Shotover, or take the consequences of not being able to pay what you owe him."

"And you don't count it underhanded to carry such a tale?"

"I do not. It would have been if I hadn't told you first. I would tell Miss Shotover, only, if she be anything of a girl, she wouldn't believe me."

"I should think not! Come, come, be reasonable! I always thought you a good sort of fellow, though I was rough on you, I confess. There! Take the money, and leave me my change."

"No. Gertrude should at least know the sort of man you are. I mean to tell the truth about you."

"Then do your worst."

Marway tried to kick him, failed, and strode into the dark between him and the lamps of the town.

Marway was a fine, handsome fellow whose manners, where he saw reason soon won him favor, and two of the young men in the office were his ready slaves. Every moment of the next day, Clare was watched. Clare could hardly do anything before the dinner-hour, but Marway would make doubly sure.

At anchor in the roads lay a certain frigate, whose duty it was to sail around the islands. Among the young officers on board were two of Marway's friends. He had met with them the night before, and they had plotted a scheme for nullifying Clare's interference which his friends also had reason to wish successful, for Marway owed them both money. Clare had come in the way of all three.

Now little Ann was a guardian cherub to the object of

their enmity, and he and she must first of all be separated. Clare had asked leave of Miss Shotover to take the child to Noah's ark, as she called it, that evening, and Marway had learned it from her: Clare's going would favor their plan, but the child's presence would render it unworkable.

One thing in their favor was that Mr. Shotover was away from home. If Clare had resolved on telling him rather than the admiral, he would not until the next evening, and that would give them abundant time. On the other hand, having him watched, they could easily prevent him from finding the admiral. But Clare had indeed come to the just conclusion that his master had the first right to know what he had to tell. His object was not the exposure of Marway, but the protection of his master's daughter: he would, therefore, wait Mr. Shotover's return. He said to himself also, that Marway would thereby have a chance to repent.

As soon as Clare had put the bank in order for the night, he went to find his little companion, and take her to Noah's ark. The child had been sitting all morning and afternoon in a profound stillness of expectation—but the hour came and passed, and Clare did not appear.

He went to the little room of the hall, where he almost always found her waiting for him. She was not there. Nobody came. He grew impatient, and ran in his eagerness up the front stair. At the top he met the butler coming from the drawing room.

"Pardon me, Mr. Porson," said the butler, who was especially polite to Clare, recognizing in him the enoblement of his own order, "but it is against the rules for any of the gentlemen below to come up this staircase."

"I know I'm in the wrong," answered Clare, "but I was in such a hurry I ventured this once. I've been waiting for Miss Ann twenty mintues."

"If you will go down, I will make inquiry, and let you know directly," replied the butler.

Clare went down, and had not waited more than another minute when the butler brought the message that the child was not to go out. In vain Clare sought an explanation: the old man knew nothing of the matter, but confessed that Miss Shotover seemed a little put out.

Then Clare saw that his desire to do justice had thwarted his endeavor: Marway had seen Miss Shotover, he concluded, and had so thoroughly prejudiced her against anything Clare might say, that she had already taken the child from him! He regretted that he had told Marway his purpose before he was ready to follow it up with immediate action. Distressed at the thought of little Ann's disappointment, he set out for the show, glad in the midst of his grief, that he was going to see the puma once more.

Clare wandered on, and the minutes passed slowly. At last, it being now quite dark, he turned, and headed for the caravans.

A crowd was going up the steps, passing Mrs. Halliwell slowly, and descending into the area surrounded by the beasts. Clare went up, and laid his money on the little white table. The good woman took it with a smile, threw it in her wooden bowl, and handed him, as if it had been his change, three bright sovereigns. Clare turned his face away. He could not take them, for it would break one bond between them.

"The money's your own!" she said, in a low voice.

"By and by, Mother!" he answered.

"No, no, take it now," she insisted, in an almost angry whisper. At the same moment she threw the sovereigns among the silver and copper coins that lay on the table.

Judging by her look that he had better say nothing, Clare turned and went down the steps. Before he reached the bottom of them, Glum Gunn elbowed his way past him, throwing a scowl on him from his ugly eyes at the range of a few inches.

The place was fuller than it had been all the evening, and with a rougher sort of company. Clare did not know that he was watched and followed by Marway, with two others, and one burly, middle-age, sailor-looking fellow.

He avoided going straight to the puma, contenting himself for the moment with an occasional glimpse of him between the moving heads. Clare hoped to get gradually nearer unseen, so he would not attract attention by becoming the object of an uproarious outbreak of the puma's affection.

But while Clare was yet a good way from him, a most ferocious yell sprang full grown into the air, which Clare knew as one of the cries of the puma when most enraged. There he was on his hind legs, ramping against the front of the cage, every hair on him bristling, his tail lashing his flanks. The same instant arose a commotion in the crowd behind Clare, a pushing and stooping and swaying to and fro, with shouts of, "Here he is! Here he is!"

Filled with foreboding, he forced his way nearer to the puma. Then, elbowing roughly through the spectators, Glum Gunn appeared, almost between him and the cage—once more, to the horror of Clare, holding by the neck his poor little Abdiel, curled up into the shape of a flea. The brute was making his way with him to the cage of the puma, whose wrath now blazed at the dog. Some waft of the wild odor of the menagerie must have reached the nostrils of Abdiel, brought back old times and his master, and waked the hope of finding him. That he had but just arrived was plain, for he had not had time to get to his master.

Clare was almost at the edge of the close-packed, staring crowd, absorbed in the sight of the huge, raving cat. Breaking through its outermost ring in the strength of sudden terror, he darted to the cage to reach it before Glum Gunn. A man crossed and hustled him. Gunn opened the door of the cage, and flung Abdiel to the puma. Before he could close it, Clare struck Gunn a stout left-hander on the side of his head. Gunn staggered back. Clare sprang into the cage—just as the puma spied him and uttered a jubilant roar of recognition. His jumping into the cage just prevented the puma from getting out, and the crowd from trampling each other to death to escape. But now that Clare was in, the cage door might have swung all night open unheeded—so long, that is, as no dog appeared.

As for Abdiel, the puma had forgotten him. The dog was out of his sight for the moment, though only behind him, while he and Clare were rubbing noses. Abdiel showed his wisdom by keeping in the background. The moment he was flung into the cage, he slunk into a corner of it, and stood up on his hind legs.

The puma's delight had broken out in wildest motion. He sprang to the roof of his cage, and grappling there, looked down and saw the dog. Poor Abdiel immediately raised his head and began a little dance his master had taught him.

Clare sprang to the rescue, and the weight of the puma's bulk descended, not on Abdiel, but on the shoulders of Clare who had the dog in his bosom. In a moment more their common love was evident. The puma forgot his hate, the dog forgot his fear, and presently, to the admiration of the crowd, Clare and the puma and the dog were rolling over and over each other on the floor of the cage.

Glum Gunn, too angry to speak, stood watching with a scowl fit for Lucifer when he rose from his first fall from heaven. He could do nothing! He would bide his time, but he would keep hold of his chance! At a moment when Clare was under the two animals, Gunn locked the cage door. He had Clare now—and his beast of a dog too!

Gunn felt a touch on his arm and glanced sullenly round. Marway, with his eye and thumb, motioned Gunn to withdraw for a moment, and he did not hesitate. As he went, he chuckled to himself at the thought of Clare when he found the door locked.

Marway's three accomplices had drifted off one by one to wait for him outside. He rejoined them with Gunn, and the five went a little way from the caravan and talked.

Clare seemed absorbed in his game with his four-footed friends, but he was wide awake. He had Abdiel to deliver, and he kept half an eye on Gunn. He saw Marway come up to him, and saw them come back together: it was the very moment to leave the cage with Abdiel! Clare rose and went to the cage door.

In vain, Clare tried to open the door. He had never known it locked, and could not think when it had been done. Amid the laughter of the spectators, he gave up, and the three resumed their frolics.

At this time, the admiration of the visitors broke out. They had seen the door fastened and had kept pretty quiet, waiting to see what would come: they had thus earned their amusement when Clare tried in vain to open it. But when they saw him laugh and all three return to their games, they applauded heartily.

Just before this last portion of the entertainment, Mr. Halliwell, who had been looking on for a while, retired, not knowing that the cage door was locked. He went to his wife and said that if they had but the boy and his dog again, and were free of that brother of his, the menagerie would be a wild-beast paradise. He would have had her go and see the pranks in the puma's cage, but she was too tired, she said. So he strolled out with his pipe, and left his men to close the exhibition. Mrs. Halliwell fastened her door and went to bed, a little hurt that Clare did not come back to see her.

Gradually, the crowd thinned out, and at last only a few people remained. One by one they shuffled out, the readier now that Clare was too tired to play with the puma and the dog. When Abdiel, not free from fear and not yet free from danger, crept to his master's bosom, the puma gave a low growl. He shoved his nose under the dog's long body, and with one jerk threw him a yard off upon the floor. Abdiel returned to content himself with his master's feet, abandoning the place of honor to the puma. So they all fell asleep in peace.

Although Clare knew himself and Abdiel to be Gunn's prisoners, he feared no surprise with two such rousable companions.

CHAPTER TWENTY-FOUR
Hope Reawakened

When Clare awoke, he knew he had been asleep a long time. It was quite dark, and there was something wrong with him. His head ached: it had never ached before. He put out his hands, but the puma's hairy body was nowhere near. He called Abdiel, but no whimper answered, and no cold nose was thrust into his hand. He had gone to sleep, surely between his two friends! Could he have only dreamed it?

Why was the darkness so thick? There must surely be light in the clouds by this time! He felt half awake and half dreaming. What was the curious motion beneath him? Could it be a gentle earthquake that was rocking him to and fro?

Clare put his hand to his face: his cheek was wet, and felt like blood! He tried to get on his feet, but as he rose, his head struck something, and he dropped back. He got on his knees again and groped about. On all sides he was closed in, but not in a dungeon of stone: he seemed to be in a great wooden box—small enough to be a box, much too large for a coffin.

What had become of Abdiel? Had Glum Gunn got him? Then the wet on his face was Abdiel's blood—shed in his defense, perhaps, when his enemies were taking him away!

Fears and anxieties, such as Clare had never known before, began to crowd upon him. Something dreadful might be going on that he could not prevent! He had never been so miserable. It was high time to do something—to ask the great One somewhere to do what ought to be done for little Ann, and Abdiel, and the puma! He prayed in his heart, lay still, and fell fast asleep.

155

He came to himself again, in the act of drawing a deep breath of cool, delicious air. He was no longer shut in the dark, stifling box. He opened his eyes and saw the strong friendly sun. He knew that he was lying on the deck of one of the great ships he had so frequently looked at from the shore. How often he had longed to travel on one of them, and now he had his heart's desire.

He lay on the ship, and the ship lay on the sea, a little world afloat on the water, moving as a planet moves through the heavens, but carrying her own heaven with her, attended by her own clouds, bearing her whither she would. Up into those clouds Clare lay gazing, up into the dome of the angels, drawing deeper and deeper breaths of gladness, too happy to think.

Then a foot came with a kick in the ribs, and a voice ordered him to get up: was he going to lie there till the frigate was paid off?

Clare scrambled to his feet, and surveyed the man who had kicked him. He had a vague sense of having seen him before, but could not remember where. Feeling faint, and finding himself beside a gun, he leaned upon it.

The sailor regarded him with an insolent look. "Wake up," he said, "an' come along to the cap'n. What's the service a comin' to, I should like to know, when a beggarly shaver like you has the cheek to stow hisself away on board one o' his majesty's frigates! Wouldn't nothin' less suit your highness than a berth on the Panther?"

"Is that the name of the ship?" asked Clare.

"Yes, that's the name of the ship!" returned the man, mimicking him. "You'll have the Panther, his mark, on the back o' you presently! Come along, I say, to the cap'n! We ha' got to ask him what's to be done wi' rascals as rob their masters, an' then stow theirselves away on board his majesty's ships!"

"Take me to the captain," said Clare.

The man seemed for a moment to doubt whether there might not be some mistake: he had expected to see Clare cringe. But he took him by the collar behind, and pushed him along to the quarterdeck, where an elderly officer was pacing up and down alone.

"Well, Tom," said the captain, stopping in his walk, "what's the matter? Who's that you've got?"

"Please, yer honor," answered the boatswain, giving Clare a shove, "this here's a stowaway. I found him snug in the cable-tier. Salute the captain, you beggar!"

Clare had no cap to lift, but he bowed like the gentleman he was. The captain stood looking at him. Clare returned his gaze, and smiled. A sort of tremble, much like that in the level air on a hot summer day, went over the captain's face, and he looked harder at Clare.

A sound arose like the purring of an enormous cat and, sure enough, it was nothing else: chained to the foot of the forward binnacle* stood a panther, a dark yellow creature with black spots, bigger than the puma, swinging his tail. The panther made a bound and leap to the height and length of his chain, and uttered a cry like a musical yawn. Clare stretched out his arms, and staggered toward him. The next moment the animal had him, and the captain darted to the rescue. But the beast was only licking him and tossing him over and over as if he were a baby, and in his vibrating body and his whole behavior manifested an exceeding joy. The captain stood staring, stunned.

The boatswain was not astonished: he had seen Clare at home among wild animals, and thought the panther was taken with the wild-beast smell about him.

"I beg your pardon, sir," said Clare, rolling himself out of the panther's reach, and rising to his feet, "but wild things like me somehow! I slept with a puma last night. He and this panther, sir, would have a terrible fight if they met!"

"Go forward, Tom," he said.

The man did not like the turn things had taken, and as he went wore something of the look of one doomed to make the acquaintance of another kind of cat.

"What made you come on board this ship, my lad?" asked

the captain, in a voice so quiet that it sounded almost kind.

"I did not come on board, sir."

"Don't trifle with me," returned the captain sternly.

Clare looked straight at him and said, "I have done nothing wrong, sir. I know you will help me. I fell asleep last night, sir, in the cage of a puma. I knew him, of course! How I came awake on board your ship, I know no more than you do, sir."

The smile of Clare's childhood had scarcely altered, and it now shone full on the captain. He turned away, and made a tack or two on the quarterdeck. He was a tall, thin man, with a graceful carriage, and a little stoop in the shoulders. He had a handsome, sad face, growing old. His hair was more than halfway gray, although he seemed about forty. He had the sternness of a man used to command, but under the sternness Clare saw the sadness.

The attention of the boy was now somewhat divided between the captain and his panther, which seemed possessed with a fiercely friendly desire to get at him. The attention of the captain seemed divided between the boy and the panther; his eyes now rested for a moment on the animal, now turned again to the boy. "What is your name?" he asked.

"I don't quite know, sir," answered Clare.

"Come with me," said the captain.

He led the way to his stateroom, and the boy followed. The panther gave a howl as Clare disappeared. The captain's lips were compressed as if with vengeance, but the muscles of his face were twitching.

CHAPTER TWENTY-FIVE
Hope Fulfilled

Clare followed, wondering, but not anxious. The captain looked a good man, and good man was a friend to Clare! But when Clare entered the stateroom and saw himself from head to foot in a mirror let into a bulkhead, he was both startled and ashamed: how could the captain take such a scarecrow into his room! He had indeed felt dirty and disreputable, and been aware of the dry, rasping tongue of the panther on many patches of bare skin, but he had had no idea how wretched he looked. Not one of the garments he saw in the mirror was his own, and they were disgracefully torn. His hair was sticking out every way, and his face smeared with blood. His feet were bare, and one trouser-leg ripped to the knee.

The captain turned and sat down. The boy stood in the doorway, staring into the mirror. The captain understood his consternation. "Come along, my poor boy," he said. "How did you get into this mess?"

"I think I know," answered Clare, "but I'm not sure."

The captain gazed at him for several moments, then said, "You say you did not come on board the frigate. What am I to understand by that?"

"That I was brought, sir, in my sleep. It wouldn't be fair, would it, sir, to mention names, when I don't know for certain who they were that brought me? I never knew anything till I opened my eyes, and thought I was in—"

He paused.

"Where did you think you were?" the captain asked.

"In the dome of the angels, sir," answered Clare.

159

The captain's face fell. He thought him an innocent, on whom rascals had been playing a practical joke. But that made no difference! If he were a simpleton, he might none the less be—! The captain shuddered visibly. "Tell me," he said, "what you remember."

He meant what Clare remembered of the circumstances that immediately preceded his coming to himself on board the Panther, but Clare began with the first thing his memory presented him with. Perhaps he was yet a little dazed. He had not gotten through a single sentence, when he saw that something earlier wanted telling first; and with the same thing happening again and again within the first five minutes of his narration, the captain, Sir Harry, saw he had before him a boy either of fertile imagination, or of a strange, eventful history. He must make him begin at the beginning and tell *everything* he knew about himself!

"Stop!" he said. "You told me you did not quite know your name. What did they call you as far back as you can remember?"

"Clare Porson," answered the boy.

At the first word the captain gave a little cry, but repressed his emotion, and went on. His face was very white, and his breath came and went quickly. "Why did you say you did not quite know your name?"

"My father and mother called me by their name because there was nobody to tell them what my real name was."

"Then they weren't your own father and mother that give you that name?"

"No, sir. I'm but using theirs till I get my own. I shall one day."

"Why do you think so?"

"Don't you think, sir, that everything will come right one day?"

"God grant it!" responded the captain with a groan, self-reproached for the little faith beside the strong desire.

"Do you think it wrong, sir, to use a name that is not quite my own?" Clare asked. "People sometimes seem to think so."

"Not at all, my boy! You must have a name. They gave it to you, and you did not steal it."

"Mr. Porson gave me his own name, and he was a clergyman. So I thought afterward, when I had to think about it, that it couldn't be wrong to use it."

"Did Mr. Porson give you *both* your names?" he asked.

"No, sir. My mother said I brought the first with me. She said I told them that my name was Clare."

The captain drove back the words that threatened to break from his lips in spite of himself.

"I mean my second mother, sir," continued Clare. "My own mother is in the dome of the angels."

A flash lightened from the captain's eyes, but he seemed to himself to have gone blind. Clare saw the flash, and wondered.

Again the dome of the angels! The words burst into meaning. Out of the depths of the world of life rose to the captain's mind's eye the terrible thing that had made him a lonely man. Again he stood with his head thrown back, looking up at the Assumption of the Virgin painted in that awful dome—again the earthquake seized the church, and shook the painted heaven down upon them. His little boy had been standing near him, holding his mother's hand, but staring up like his father!

He had to force the next words from his throat. "Where did the good people who gave you their name find you?"

"Sitting on my mother—my own mother. The angels fell down on her, and when they went up again, she had got mixed with them, and went up too."

The stern, sorrowful man hid his face in his hands. "Grace," he murmured—and Clare knew somehow that he spoke to his wife, "we have him again! We will never distrust Him more!" And his frame heaved with choking sobs.

Then Clare understood that the grand man was his father. The awe of a perfect gladness fell upon him. He knelt before him, and laid his hands together as in prayer.

"Why did you distrust me, Father?" asked the half-naked outcast.

"It was not my child; it was my Father I distrusted. I am ashamed," said Sir Harry, and clasped Clare in his arms.

The boy laid his blood-stained face against his father's bosom, and his soul was in a better home than a sky full of angels, a home better than the dome itself of all the angels, for his home was his father's heart.

The father relaxed at length the arms that strained his child to his heart. Clare looked up and gazed at his father, cried like little Ann, "You've come!" and slid to his feet. He clasped and kissed and clung to them—would hardly let them go.

All this time the officers on the quarterdeck were wondering what the captain could have to do with the beggarly stowaway. The panther stood on his feet, anxiously waiting, his ears starting at every sound. He was longing for the boy with whom he had played, panther cub with human infant, in the years long gone by. The two were the same age, and had rolled on the ship's floor and deck together when neither could hurt—and now neither would.

Sir Harry raised his son, kissed him, set him on his own chair, and stepped into an inner cabin. A knock came to the door, and Clare said, "Come in." The quartermaster entered, and saw the miserable stowaway seated in the captain's chair. He swore at him and ordered him out.

"The captain told me to sit here," answered Clare.

The officer looked closer at him, begged his pardon, saluted, and withdrew. The captain heard, and said to himself, "The boy is a gentleman: he knows where to take his orders." Then he called Clare to him and washed him from head to foot.

"Now what are we to do for clothes, Clare?" said Sir Harry.

"Perhaps somebody would lend me some," answered Clare. "Mayn't I be your cabin boy, Father? You will let me be a sailor, won't you, and sail always with you?"

"You shall be a sailor, my boy," answered Sir Harry, "and sail with me as long as God pleases."

"I will obey the cook if you tell me, Father."

"You shall obey nobody but me—and the lord high admiral," he added, with a glance upward, and a smile like his son's.

The next day Clare went on deck in a midshipman's uniform, which he wore like a gentleman that could obey orders.

His father had a hammock slung for him in the stateroom; he could not be parted from him even when they slept.

One night Sir Harry, laying awake, heard a movement in the stateroom, and got up. It was a still, starlit night. The frigate was dreaming away northward with all sails set. Through the windows shone the level stars. From a beam above hung a dim lamp. He could see no one, and went to the hammock. There was no boy in it. Then he spied him, kneeling under the stern-windows, with his head down.

"Anything the matter, Clare?" he asked.

"No, Father, I'm only trying to say *Thank You* for my father!"

"Oh, thank Him, thank Him, my boy!" returned Sir Harry. "Thank Him with all your heart. He will give us *her* someday!"

"Yes, Father, He will!" responded Clare.

His father knelt beside him, but neither said a word that the other heard.

The next night Clare was on the quarterdeck with his father. It was gusty and dark, threatening foul weather. The captain walked the quarterdeck as slowly and stately as before, but with a look almost of triumph in his eyes, glancing often at the clouds. The thought of having such a father made Clare tremble with delight. His father was the power of the ship that bore them! The great vessel and all aboard her obeyed *him!* At his pleasure she bowed her obedient head, and swept over the seas! Clare's heart swelled within him.

But this father had, the night before, knelt with Clare in the presence of One unseen, worshiping and thanking One higher than himself. As the captain of the Panther sailed his frigate through the seas, so the great Father to whom the captain knelt as a little child, sailed through the heaven of heavens the huge ship of the world. And over an infinitely grander sea the Father was carrying navies of human souls, every soul a world whose affairs none but the Father could understand, through many a storm and battle with the powers of evil, safe to the haven of the children, the Father's house! And Clare began to understand that so it was.

One day his father said to him, "Clare, whatever you forget, whatever you remember, mind this—that you and I and your mother are the children of one Father, and that we have all three to be good children to that Father. If we do as He tells us, He will bring us all at length to the same port. Our admiral is Jesus Christ, and we take our orders from Him."

Clare worked to become a sailor, and he learned fast. He was as precise in obeying any superior officer as the best sailor aboard. In a few weeks he felt and looked to the manner born—as indeed he was, for not only his father, but his grandfather, and his great-grandfather, and more yet of his ancestors, had been sailors.

Clare had had a rough shaking. The earthquake had come and gone, and come again and gone many times. But the shaking earth was his nurse, and she taught him to dwell in a world that cannot be shaken.

AFTERWORD

MacDonald's story of Clare Skymer ends here, abruptly it seems. Perhaps he intended to write a sequel to tell the rest of Clare's life story—his life at sea, in the desert, and how he came to live at last in a quiet country village.

What happened to all the other people and animals?

We know from a few scattered clues in the original story that Clare and his father were many weeks at sea and visited many ports before they came once again to the harbor where they had been reunited. And we know that Clare returned to find Ann, who told him, "You never, never, never came. I had to go to bed, and the beasts went away."

And we know that he returned to claim the baby he had rescued from the water barrel—that she grew up and married a Mr. Waterhouse, and became Clare's housekeeper.

As for the rest? We can only guess. Perhaps Clare returned to find the faithful Abdiel wounded, but safe and recovering at Miss Tempest's. Abdiel probably spent the rest of his life with Clare, and became the ancestor of many of Clare's beloved dogs (including Tadpole).

And Ann? She had been waiting for Clare all her life, just as Clare had been waiting for his father. It's likely that Clare grew up, and waited for her to grow up, and then married her—and the little awe-struck boy who opened the gate for Clare was their grandson.

bandbox: A long, round box used to hold lightweight items of clothing.

bartering: Trading or exchanging one thing for another of similar value.

bellows: A pleated, expandable tool that takes in air through a valve and lets it out through a tube; a blower. A blacksmith used a bellows to blow on a fire and keep the coals alive.

binnacle: a case, box, or stand containing a ship's compass and lamp.

chancery: A high court of justice in Great Britain.

coves: Another way of referring to men or fellows.

draper: A merchant who sells cloth and clothing and sometimes other dry goods.

festa: A celebration held each year to honor the local patron saint.

haberdasher: A merchant who sells small items.

half-crown: A British coin with two shillings and sixpence.

hiding: A severe spanking.

lockup: The local jail.

mizzle: To depart suddenly.

omnibus: A bus or public vehicle designed to carry a large number of passengers.

page: A boy hired to run errands and deliver messages.

pence: Plural for penny. At the time this story was written, 240 pence were equal in value to one pound.

piazza: An open square or porch.

pound: A British monetary unit.

scullery: A room near a kitchen used for cleaning and storing dishes, washing vegetables, and other such tasks.

seeress: A woman who can predict the future.

shilling: A British coin equal to twelve pence or 1/20 pound.

sovereign: A British coin containing 113 grains of gold and equal in value to one pound.

workhouse: The poorhouse; a place of correction for people who have broken the law.

Winner Books are produced by Victor Books and are designed to entertain and instruct young readers in Christian principles.

Other Winner Books you will enjoy:
The Mystery Man of Horseshoe Bend
    by Linda Boorman
The Drugstore Bandit of Horseshoe Bend
    by Linda Boorman
The Hairy Brown Angel and Other Animal Tails
    edited by Grace Fox Anderson
The Peanut Butter Hamster and Other Animal Tails
    edited by Grace Fox Anderson
Skunk for Rent and Other Animal Tails
    edited by Grace Fox Anderson
The Incompetent Cat and Other Animal Tails
    edited by Grace Fox Anderson
The Duck Who Had Goosebumps and Other Animal Tails
    edited by Grace Fox Anderson
The Mysterious Prowler by Frances Carfi Matranga
The Forgotten Treasure by Frances Carfi Matranga
The Mystery of the Missing Will by Frances Carfi Matranga
The Hair-Pulling Bear Dog by Lee Roddy
The City Bear's Adventures by Lee Roddy
Dooger, the Grasshopper Hound by Lee Roddy
The Ghost Dog of Stoney Ridge by Lee Roddy
Mad Dog of Lobo Mountain by Lee Roddy
The Legend of the White Raccoon by Lee Roddy
The Boyhood of Ranald Bannerman
    by George MacDonald
The Genius of Willie MacMichael by George MacDonald
The Wanderings of Clare Skymer by George MacDonald